the great **ceviche** book

the great ceviche book

revised

Douglas Rodriguez

with Laura Zimmerman

Photography by Christopher Hirsheimer and Chugrad McAndrews

TEN SPEED PRESS
Berkeley

Library of Congress Cataloging-in-Publication Data
Rodriguez, Douglas.
  The great ceviche book / Douglas Rodriguez with
Laura Zimmerman ; photography by Christopher
Hirsheimer and Chugrad McAndrews ; [foreword
by Calvin Trillin]. — Rev. ed.
    p. cm.
  Includes index.
  1. Cookery (Seafood) 2. Cookery (Cold dishes)
3. Cookery, Latin American. I. Zimmerman,
Laura. II. Title.
  TX747.R635 2010
  641.598—dc22

                                    2009049570

ISBN 978-1-58008-107-8

Printed in China

Design by Toni Tajima
Food and prop styling on pages vi, 6, 9, 21, 43,
76, 85 by Jenny Martin-Wong
Props used in remaining photographs courtesy of
Apartment 48 Home Furnishings, New York
Seafood used in remaining photographs courtesy
of Pacifica International and M. Slavin & Sons,
New York

10 9 8 7 6 5 4 3

Revised Edition

To my partner in life,

Nelly Olga Gracia,

with love, respect,

and admiration.

I wouldn't be anywhere

without your inspiration.

CONTENTS

ACKNOWLEDGMENTS

Inspiration may come to you in many different ways.

But most often it comes to me in my travels, away from my day to day routine—when I'm in a relaxed mode. Often this happens when I take culinary trips with other chefs, friends, colleagues, and employees.

So first I would like thank my chefs, colleagues, and employees—those who keep my creative wheels turning. Chef Jose-Luis Flores, thank you for your friendship, loyalty, and inspiration. I would like to thank Roberto Madrid, Darren Carbone, David Laforce, and Horacio Riveradero for their support.

I also want to give thanks to those who are on their own: Jose Garces (the Iron Chef), Raymond Mohan, Ramiro Jimenez, Maximo Tejeda, and Adrian Leon.

As always, Felipe Rojas Lombardi, who inspired me from an early age and taught me the power of spreading the word of the Latin table.

My editor, Annie Nelson, and all my friends at Ten Speed Press. A special thanks to Phil Wood, for his patience, gentle pressure, and encouragement in this, my fourth book. May our adventures together allow for more storytelling and idea sharing.

Christopher Hirsheimer and Chugrad McAndrews, for contributing the beautiful photographs for this book.

Laura Zimmerman, my coauthor, for researching, organizing, and fine-tuning the text and putting my voice so accurately into written words.

Dr. Joe Regenstein, of Cornell University's Food Science Department, and Dr. Robert Price, of the University of California, Davis's Food Science and Technology Department, for furthering my knowledge of seafood safety, specifically in reference to home preparation.

Many of my chef friends and seafood suppliers across the country who helped me put together the very useful seafood sources guide in the back of this book.

My mom, my dad, and my brother, Frank, for their love and support and many good times around the dinner table.

My kids, Victoria, Leandro, and Dario, who are happy to eat mac and cheese. Hopefully one day you guys will eat ceviche.

FOREWORD by Calvin Trillin

Douglas Rodriguez is not someone you could accuse of lacking enthusiasm for his calling.

The first time I went to see him, what I had in mind was simply getting some suggestions about where to eat ceviche. I had no idea that he was going to get himself all worked up. A few years before this, I had spent some time in Ecuador, and to say that I'd become fond of Ecuadorian ceviche would be like saying that Gauguin, when he got to Tahiti, found himself reasonably impressed by the native women. When I began planning a return to that part of South America in order to do an article on ceviche, I figured it made sense to begin by consulting with the man who, first at Patria and then at Chicama, had brought ceviche into the Manhattan mainstream.

Douglas and I were sitting at a table at Chicama, which, he reminded me, had been named for a coastal village in Peru, a country whose ceviche is sometimes thought of as rather formal or even stately. Then he started talking about Peruvian ceviche, which is chunks of cured fish and spices and onions, always flanked by wedges of potato or corn. As he warmed to the subject, he moved from the classic Peruvian ceviche to *tiradito*—a form of the dish in which the fish is cut into slices, more or less like sashimi. That got him into a description of the man he considered the master of Peruvian ceviche, a legendary Lima chef named Humberto Sato. Douglas discussed Sato with something approaching reverence, as if discussing some sort of Zen master, and when he told me I'd have to visit Sato's restaurant, Costanera 700, he fairly glowed with the memory of his own most recent meal there.

Then Douglas got started on the ceviche of Ecuador, which sounded like his favorite, since he seemed to become even more animated as he described how it differed from the ceviche in Peru. Like ceviche elsewhere in Latin America, Ecuadorian ceviche is made by curing fresh fish in the juice of a particularly acid lemon. Unlike any ceviche I'd had before I visited Ecuador, though, it includes enough of the curing juices to be sort of liquid; it's served in a bowl rather than on a plate. Large roasted kernels of Andean corn are served on the side, to be tossed in for both flavor and crunch. Some restaurants offer as accompaniment not only roasted corn kernels but popcorn.

Douglas mentioned some restaurants in Quito and Guayaquil, but quickly moved on to Salinas, on Ecuador's westernmost coast. He got more and more excited as he talked about the clusters of cevicherias and particularly a place called La Lojanita, whose ceviche was of such high quality, he said, that the proprietor had been elected mayor. As he described La Lojanita—or Mecca, as he sometimes called it—he was getting more and more excited. Finally, he paused for a moment, nodded his head as if he'd just come to a decision and practically shouted, "I'm going with you!"

He did. Or, at least, our parties met up in Guayaquil, and, for a few days become what I referred to in the article as the ceviche gang, an eating posse of seven or eight people moving through a section of western Ecuador cevicherias. By the time we finally reached La Lojanita, only three or four of us still felt capable of bellying up to its counter, but Douglas's order didn't seem to be affected by the reduced number of eaters. In front of us were about twenty bowls of ceviche. In my memory of that moment at La Lojanita, Douglas is praising the octopus while reaching for the black clam and questioning the countermen closely on whether we've missed anything. He had gotten himself all worked up.

INTRODUCTION

It was seventeen years ago when I first truly discovered ceviche.

Sure, I had cooked ceviches before, toyed around with different ceviche ingredients, and served ceviches to diners at my Miami restaurants. But it was in Salinas, Ecuador, in 1993 (led by my friend Humberto Mata) that I realized ceviche was not just a small snack playing a minor role at the Latin table, but a whole new culinary frontier awaiting discovery.

Sitting in the open air of La Lojanita, a cevicheria a few blocks away from the Pacific Ocean, I stared at the colorful array of no less than fifteen ceviches spread out before me. The map of flavors made my mouth water and my mind race; there were bites of delicately white merluza swirled with lime and jalapeños, chewy lobster chunks paired with bitter orange and slivers of cilantro, and buttery tuna drizzled with lemon and garnished with salty corn nuts. I was definitely inspired. Never before had I seen so many ceviche renditions served at one time, nor tasted as many variations on the seafood-and-citrus theme at one sitting. I still refer to La Lojanita as "Mecca," because it made me a convert and true believer in the importance of ceviche's role in Latin cuisine.

When I returned to New York City from Ecuador in 1994, I kept things simple, at least for a while. I opened Patria, my first restaurant

venture in the Big Apple. There I began with just three ceviches on the menu, in contrasting hues of white, red, and black: a Honduran fire and ice ceviche made of silky tuna bathed in lime and coconut milk, peppered with ginger and jalapeño, and dramatically presented in a coconut shell with pillars of fried plantain; an Ecuadorian Shrimp ceviche (page 63) flavored with roasted tomatoes, red bell pepper purée, and sweet orange and lime juices; and a Peruvian Black Ceviche (page 66), mixed with seafood flavored with squid ink to mimic the black clams I had tasted in a Peruvian ceviche. These ceviches quickly became favorites on Patria's menu, and I could sense that I was onto something.

During my five years as the Executive Chef and Owner of Patria restaurant, my thoughts often returned to that map of ceviche flavors I'd tasted in Ecuador and slowly I began to reconstruct the flavors in my head, hoping to breathe into them, someday, the life of America's bounty and my own creativity. I knew the proposition of centering a restaurant's concept around ceviche, a little-known dish already plagued by the inevitable raw-fish safety issues, was risky. But I was passionate about the idea and I knew that if it was going to work at all, my best hope was to try it in New York City. At that table in Salinas, I had seen ceviche in a whole new light, and I hoped to bring about that same awakening in my customers.

So with the new millennium, Chicama was born, in New York's Union Square neighborhood. Named after a small fishing village north of Lima, Peru, Chicama was where I took my well-marinated ideas about ceviche and translated them into real-life dishes. Of course, the menu at Chicama was not only ceviche. Rather, it was a unique combination of tastes from Central and northern South America—rich, powerful tastes pleasantly balanced by the light, cooling effects of ceviche. Still, ceviche did act as the core of Chicama, both literally and figuratively. Specialized ceviche chefs stood within a rectangular display of glistening crushed ice, colorful bowls of *mixtos* ceviches, and whole fresh fish. High stools lined the perimeter, enabling diners to watch the action, much like the design of a sushi bar.

And just like that, a craze was ignited. I fed my friends and told them about my passion for ceviche and they did the same with their friends. The ceviche revolution had taken form.

defining ceviche

At this point, it's time to start delving into the definition of ceviche. Generally speaking, ceviche is any mixture of fish or shellfish that is "cooked" by the acid of a citrus marinade (although my shellfish additions are often blanched or sautéed before marinating) and typically enhanced with chiles, onions, and cilantro. It is an ideally straightforward dish for today's style of eating, one that relies primarily on the highest-quality ingredients and skillfully precise, simple preparation rather than over-the-top creativity or elaborate, strongly flavored sauces or spices.

As the seafood in a ceviche marinates, anywhere from a few minutes to a few hours, it loses its translucent appearance, becomes firm, and absorbs flavor. Garnishes are often a critical part of the preparation of a ceviche and vary by region. For example, typical Ecuadorian accompaniments are popped corn and *cancha* (corn nuts), while Peruvians add sweet potatoes, lettuce, and ears of corn to the mix.

Don't confuse ceviche with escabeche, a similar marinated fish dish (also made with chicken, vegetables, and game) that includes citrus and vinegar and sometimes pickling spices for a sweet and sour taste. The most obvious difference between fish escabeche and ceviche is that the fish in escabeche is sautéed before being marinated, although it is still traditionally served cold or at room temperature. In my opinion, both ceviche and escabeche evolved out of the same ancient necessity to preserve food with an acidic sauce.

Ceviche is by no means a new culinary creation. Variations of the dish have actually been around for centuries in many Central and South American countries. In Peru, the Quechua highlanders of Inca times originally made ceviche-like dishes with only jewels from the sea, chiles, salt, and herbs. Some of these early preparations included a marinade of chicha, made from corn, or the acidic tumbo fruit, but it wasn't until after Spanish colonization that the citrus flavors of Seville oranges and lemons, as well as onions, became part of Peruvian interpretations of the dish. The further influence of Peru's Chinese and Japanese immigrants, who came to the country in 1849 and 1899 respectively, can be seen in many of today's ceviches, which sometimes include such ingredients as ginger and soy sauce.

Although many historians believe that the Peruvians were the first to prepare ceviche (including my mentor, Felipe Rojas-Lombardi, whose *The Art of South American Cooking* inspired some of my first experiences in the kitchen), others argue that the seafood dish originated in Ecuador, Polynesia, or even Arabia. Regardless of its birthplace, the most plentiful examples of ceviche are now found in Peru, Ecuador, and Chile. But variations can also be tasted in the coastal towns of Mexico, the Caribbean, and the rest of Central and South America. The name "ceviche" actually originated from the word *cebiche*, meaning "fish stew," and the Spanish and Latin roots *cebo* (fodder, bait) and *cibus* (food), respectively, but you'll also find it spelled "seviche" or "cebiche."

As a true ceviche lover, I, of course, have my own simple theory about the dish's origin—all tying back to the immediacy of eating a day's catch and the need to preserve food in the absence of refrigeration. Regardless of the debate over ceviche's founding country, I think the honors should logically go to a fisherman who, having limes on board his boat (to treat the common sea ailment scurvy), quickly tossed together the first ceviche.

It was in the cevicherias that line the Pacific Coast, from Argentina north to Mexico, that the idea of ceviche as a meal in and of itself was first born; where the array of ceviches I experienced during my enlightening trip to Ecuador is not a rarity, but rather a joyful fact of everyday life. It is quite common for friends to recharge after long nights of partying by relaxing over a table of fiery yet cooling ceviches and ice-cold beer. In this instance, ceviche functions not only as a satisfying cure for hunger pangs, but a refreshingly appropriate medicine after one too many drinks. You see, ceviche juice, or *leche de tigre* (tiger's milk), is alleged to cure hangovers.

General knowledge of ceviche outside the Latin community first spread across the United States in the late 1980s, when the flavors of the Caribbean filtered into Florida via the drama of New World Cuisine. Since then, ceviche's evolution has continued on Latin-inspired menus from Miami to New York to San Francisco. But I'd only call these American ceviche appearances small uprisings—nothing like the revolution that I suspect is about to come.

the virtues of ceviche

There are many reasons that I feel so passionate and confident about the future of ceviche. One is that ceviche is in keeping with the food world's return to a simpler cuisine, a cuisine that focuses on the virtue of freshness. The goal in cooking today is to capture tastes, whether from land or sea, as close to their source as possible, bringing them to the table without the interference of unnatural substances, excessive handling, or unnecessary time. In this context, a ceviche revolution makes perfect sense. As I said, the dish's very invention was born out of fishermen's desire to eat their catch straight from the sea.

Additionally, ceviche has the same health-conscious allure of sushi, which has enjoyed a revolution of its own over the past fifteen or so years. I suspect it won't be too long before consumers start seeing containers of ceviche right next to the lines of California rolls in their grocer's refrigerated cases. Ceviche has a vibrant and refreshing taste of the ocean. It is light, yet highly flavored, and it offers a guilt-free indulgence that combines high protein with minimal fat and carbohydrates. This, along with today's improved access to high-quality products, including extremely fresh seafood and more precise handling techniques, has bolstered ceviche's appeal and will continue to do so in the years to come.

Finally, I tend to think that food, in general, has the power to cut across a wide range of ethnicities, races, classes, and backgrounds, and ceviche is no exception. Rather, it is a glowing example of how a dish can often be greater than the sum of its parts and have consequences far beyond the simple need to eat; ceviche brings people together. One thing that always troubles me when visiting Latin countries is the drastically visible wealth disparity. But have a twenty-minute conversation with any inhabitant, from a tin-roofed community to a luxury high-rise, and, guaranteed, you'll receive an invitation for a home-cooked meal, likely including ceviche. In Ecuador and Peru, everyone eats ceviche, and its appeal cuts across ethnic and economic lines. Through my restaurants and this cookbook I hope to continue experiencing the pleasure of watching ceviche bring smiles to as wide a variety of American faces as possible.

basic formula

More than twenty years ago, when I began experimenting with Nuevo Latino cuisine, my logic was to begin with straightforward classic tastes and add new ethnic influences and artistic flair, without disrupting the integrity of any of the original cuisines. I followed this same logic in the creation of my ceviches. Some of the simpler, classic preparations in this book have only six ingredients, while the layered flavors of more complex recipes may have as many as twenty. Still, most of my creations here hark back to classic ideas and flavor combinations, although I always try to throw in a dash of the unexpected.

In this book, I've tried to present a compendium of variations on the ceviche theme. This should provide you with enough versions of the dish to encourage you to serve ceviche not only in its traditional role as a starter or light snack, but also as an entire meal.

As I'm sure you'll soon discover, the possibilities are really endless. As with any cooked seafood preparation, inspiration for a ceviche can come from anywhere, even a single ingredient. The exciting and unique thing about ceviche is that you experience each fish in its raw state, where its flavor is drastically different from its cooked counterpart. Essentially, you get to enjoy a totally new category of seafood tastes.

Remember that all the same culinary theories regarding the balance of texture and flavor that apply to cooked food also work for ceviche: contrast the smoothness of pompano with the delicate crunch of sea salt; the mellowness of fresh snapper with pungent culantro and sweet/sour tangerine; balance the herbal freshness of minted diver scallops with smoky bacon.

For the most part, my recipes have a relaxed style, where cooking times and ingredient lists are straightforward. When an unusual ingredient or unfamiliar fish is used, I've discussed it in the recipe introduction to tease your senses and calm your kitchen anxiety. You'll find that after your first few ceviche-making adventures, the dish is one that lends itself easily to beginners' creative whims. Conquer the basic formula, and you'll soon be sailing your own ship.

Although ceviche may inspire countless creative interpretations, the basic formula has five main ingredients besides its core of fresh fish or shellfish or an occasional vegetable or meat base. These all-important components are citrus, salt, onions, herbs, and chiles. Although I've taken many liberties with ceviche's basic formula to create the exciting dishes in this book, most of my recipes still include each of these staple ingredients. Some of the most enjoyable ceviches, such as some of the oceanside-cevicheria versions I've tasted in Ecuador, are a simple matter of tossing the day's catch, just minutes out of the water, with lime, sliced red onion, cilantro, and chiles.

Let's explore the essential components of ceviche. Understanding their role and the varieties from which to choose will give you confidence when making the recipes in this book and allow you to begin your own experimentation at home.

CITRUS

Limes and Seville, or bitter, oranges are the citrus fruits most traditionally used in ceviche, although any citrus fruit will work. However, the acidic action that "cooks" the seafood is a critical component of ceviche and thus some addition of lime, the most acidic of the citrus fruits, is essential. It is the acid in citrus that

breaks down the seafood's protein and turns it opaque, giving it a cooked appearance. In Latin America, the criollo, or yellow lime, is the citrus fruit most often used in ceviche. We know its seedless variety here in the United States as the Key lime.

You'll notice in my recipes that I have used all kinds of citrus combinations, and even sometimes sweeten my ceviche marinades with other fruits such as pineapple. Lime in any combination with grapefruit, tangerine, or orange is also a great marriage. Squeeze your citrus fruits just before adding them to any ceviche, not far in advance, as the acid in the juice will dissipate as soon as it is exposed to air.

SALT

You might be surprised to hear that salt is one of the ceviche ingredients I find most exciting to experiment with. Most consumers are only familiar with standard table salt, but there are many different kinds of salt aside from common iodized varieties, and each one varies in taste, texture, and the ease with which it dissolves. Salt is so critical to all cooking and ceviche, especially the more straightforward preparations in "Tiraditos." The simple ceviches in that chapter are a great backdrop for experiencing different salt varieties. Varying the type of salt used in a ceviche can have a marked effect on the dish. And although I typically instruct you to just use "salt" in my recipes, I encourage you to experiment and have fun.

You can splurge for *fleur de sel*, or "flower of salt," from the natural salt fields of Brittany, France, where artisan salt harvesters sweep away this clean, sweet-tasting seasoning straight from evaporated sea water. For a more economical but similar choice, try coarse kosher sea salt. I like it because its large grains sparkle like little diamonds on plates of ceviche. However, kosher salt dissolves rather quickly, so it won't hold its texture as long as *fleur de sel* does if it's mixed directly into a ceviche marinade. Try just sprinkling some on top, almost like a garnish. For a more powerful ceviche, I might even try using black sea salt, which adds a rich, slightly eggy flavor due to its high sulfur content.

ONIONS

Onions add a certain sharpness to ceviche that I think is a pleasant U-turn for your taste buds after the initial shock of the dish's acidity. When you first take a spoonful of ceviche, your mouth will pick up the refreshing citrus followed by the sharp flavor and crunch of onion. I've never seen a ceviche outside of the United States without a topping of slivered onions, typically first soaked in ice water to impart crispness and to mellow their flavor. Red onions are most often used since they possess the most powerful taste compared with the white variety, but as with all the basic ceviche ingredients, feel free to deviate from the traditional. In addition to red onion, many of this book's recipes include shallots, green onions, or chives.

HERBS

The most common herb used in ceviche is cilantro, although you will also find Peruvian huacatay, a black mint, or culantro, a robust, flat-leafed cilantro. Although the herbs used in ceviche vary somewhat by country, cilantro or one of its varieties is the most common for both its taste and its intoxicating fragrance. Herbs supplement the fresh-tasting nature of ceviche while adding another dimension of flavor. Just about any herb—oregano, parsley, basil, or mint—will work. But always use fresh herbs, never the dried variety.

CHILES

With the freshness of herbs and citrus and the pungency of onion, ceviche needs a little heat to balance its composition, hence the chile peppers at its core. From fiery Scotch bonnets to mild jalapeños and even sweet bells, peppers add a surprise kick that enlivens ceviche's silky seafood and clean citrus flavors and textures. The more traditional *aji*, or pepper, additions include amarillo, rocoto, panca, and chile limo, a tiny red pepper from Peru with a citrusy overtone. But since these aren't readily available in American groceries, any choice from the chile world will work just fine, including jalapeños. One of my favorite ways to add jalapeños to ceviche is to pickle them first (see page 111), marinating the thin red and green pepper slices with vinegar, sugar, and salt. The pickling tames the heat of the peppers and produces a condiment that is terrific on ceviche or just about anything. I use these in many of my ceviche recipes.

GARNISHES AND SIDE DISHES

Although not one of the five core ingredients, garnishes are a critical part of eating ceviches. Many garnishes, such as popcorn and corn nuts, act to cleanse the palate, cutting through the acid of the ceviche and readying the mouth for another bite of new flavor. Other garnishes, such as ears of *mote* (giant Peruvian white corn) or roasted *camote* (sweet potato), add substance and make ceviche a meal in and of itself. Still others, such as coconut milk, sliced avocado, or a drizzle of olive or sesame oil, impart an added level of richness and flavor. I choose appropriate garnishes for each ceviche by using the same theory that I do for constructing the ceviche recipe itself: choose pairings that offer texture, taste, and color contrasts. Smooth, creamy-white scallops finished with a crispy note of crumbled bacon, and silky, coral-colored sea urchin topped with delicately crunchy carrots and purple shallots are both perfect marriages of flavors and textures.

Side dishes work in a similar way, helping to enliven and extend lighter ceviche preparations while tempering the complexity of more robust recipes. I've dedicated an entire chapter to sides that complement the many ceviches in this book. An intricate ceviche, like the Paella Ceviche full of shellfish and saffron on page 62, works perfectly as its own meal with a simple side of grilled corn, while the more streamlined flavors of the Grouper with Opal Basil (page 28) pair better with Papas Huancaina (page 83), Yukon Gold potatoes covered with a creamy cheese sauce rich with eggs and milk. Just as a piece

of cheese is a perfect accompaniment to a glass of wine, rich side dishes are often an ideal balance to ceviche's crisp, pure flavors.

ceviche safety: the four commandments

One of the challenges I knew I would face in publishing this book was overcoming consumer concern about the safety of eating homemade ceviche. With the current widespread appeal of sushi, most of us who enjoy raw seafood preparations have become fairly comfortable eating them in our local restaurants. We've learned how to choose establishments that we can trust, and the associated health risks usually don't warrant so much as an afterthought. However, preparing ceviche in the home can be quite different than preparing it in a professional kitchen and may make even the most experienced home cooks a bit guarded. Following are a few tips to help ensure top-quality purchasing and safe handling in your kitchen, so you can confidently enjoy the ceviches in this book. These recommendations mirror many of those supported by the Food and Drug Administration.

KNOW YOUR FISHMONGER

Just as you wouldn't order carry-out sushi from a restaurant you hadn't seen, don't purchase fresh seafood without carefully looking around at your fishmonger's facilities and employees. Mostly, just be aware and use your common sense. Look for:

- Clean employees wearing and changing disposable gloves for each raw seafood purchase.
- Seafood displayed over plentiful fresh ice. Avoid prepackaged fish, as packaging makes it difficult to determine its freshness and whether it's been previously frozen.
- A well-maintained facility that looks and smells clean.
- A knowledgeable fishmonger who is open to questions and can talk to you about the freshness of the seafood.
- A good reputation. Ask around and only buy from reputable sources.

KNOW HOW TO IDENTIFY FRESH FISH

Knowledge is power, and if you know what to look for when purchasing seafood, you have the power to pick the choicest products—a key to making safe and delicious ceviche. Make sure the fish you purchase has the following qualities:

- Firm and shiny flesh that springs back when pressed.
- No brown or yellowish discoloration.
- A clean smell with no trace of fishiness or ammonia.
- Full, clear eyes and bright red gills free of slime (if purchasing whole fish).

KNOW YOURSELF

Unfortunately, there are some people who are more susceptible to the risks of eating raw seafood and need to refrain from the pleasures of ceviche. In general, these are extremely young children, elderly adults, pregnant women, and any severely immune-deficient individuals. If you fall under one of these demographics, err on the side of extreme caution.

KNOW YOUR KITCHEN

Once you've acquired the freshest seafood possible for your ceviche, safe handling in your own kitchen is extremely important. Follow these guidelines:

- Purchase seafood the same day you plan to make ceviche.
- Place the seafood in your refrigerator immediately after purchasing it.
- Use clean hands, cutlery, countertops, cutting boards, bowls, and other utensils to prepare raw seafood and separate those used to prepare raw seafood from those used for other ingredients, such as the citrus, onions, herbs, and chiles typical in ceviche.
- Always marinate ceviche covered in the refrigerator, never at room temperature.

Now that those tips are out of the way, you should know that, contrary to popular belief, eating raw seafood is no more risky than eating, say, cooked chicken or pork. In fact, according to a National Academy of Sciences' report on seafood safety and the Food and Drug Administration/Center for Disease Control Risk Assessment, eating seafood (including raw shellfish) is actually ten times safer than eating cooked chicken. Additionally, the risks associated with eating seafood are almost always (nearly 85 percent of the time, as estimated by the FDA) associated with the consumption of raw molluscan shellfish. In this book, I typically recommend cooking shellfish, such as mussels or clams, before adding them to ceviche.

Freezing can also ensure safe consumption because it kills parasites, so the freezing method I recommend for thinly slicing certain seafoods, including diver scallops and spiny lobster, will also aid safe eating. Still, there are a few members of the shellfish family that really should be enjoyed raw, like sea urchin and oysters. But if you're the type of diner who's too worried about food safety to enjoy the cool, briny flavor of a freshly shucked oyster, you're probably not reading this book.

The citrus juice and salt contained in all ceviche recipes do make ceviche slightly safer than sushi or sashimi, even though these ingredients do not technically cook the fish. Out of all of these considerations, the true key begins with precisely following my previous recommendations on safe purchasing and handling.

basic equipment

Ceviche is a remarkably low-tech dish to make. There are, however, a few basic pieces of equipment that will help you efficiently prepare ceviche:

VERY SHARP KNIFE

Many of the preparations in this book call for slicing seafood very thinly. Even if you use my suggested method of freezing certain seafoods before slicing, a very sharp knife is still necessary to get the job done safely and accurately. A sharp blade will allow you to easily cut through the seafood, making beautiful, delicate slices while keeping the flesh of the fish intact. A blunt knife will likely mangle the flesh and result in subpar presentation and texture. I recommend a 10-inch chef's knife. Use one in which the blade and handle are of balanced weight,

so that your hand does not tire while working. Check the balance by holding the knife where the blade and handle come together. The knife shouldn't dip in either direction, but remain level.

JAPANESE MANDOLINE

A mandoline is a rectangular slicing board with an adjustable blade for cutting various ingredients. I may recommend using a mandoline in a particular recipe if I want vegetable ingredients to be sliced extremely thinly or cut into julienne strips. Of course, you can always do this preparation by hand, but the mandoline makes all the slicing and dicing much more enjoyable and uniform. I prefer a plastic Japanese mandoline. You can find them in most kitchen equipment supply stores. Just be extremely careful when using a mandoline. The repetitive and quick slicing motion can easily cause you to lose track of the distance between your fingers and the blade. Most mandolines come with a useful hand guard. If yours does not, use a kitchen towel to protect your hand when you're first getting used to this tool.

CUTTING BOARD

Use a heavy, thick plastic cutting board that won't move around easily while you're preparing your ceviche ingredients. I recommend against wood cutting boards because the fish aromas can penetrate the wood and are difficult to wash away. I find that plastic is not as porous and washes clean particularly well.

CITRUS REAMER

Freshly squeezed citrus juice is one of the most critical elements of ceviche and an essential ingredient of ceviche's basic formula. Using a wooden, handheld citrus reamer is quick and allows you to add some juicy bits of citrus pulp into the ceviche marinade.

NONREACTIVE BOWL

A nonreactive glass or stainless steel mixing bowl is essential for marinating ceviche so that the fish does not pick up any flavor from the bowl, metallic or otherwise.

serving suggestions

Here are a handful of suggestions for serving ceviche to guests. Note that the key is keeping ceviche cold; the colder the better. Making temperature a priority ensures a light and refreshing dish.

CHILLED MARTINI GLASSES

Martini glasses are dramatic and can easily be frosted in your home freezer to hold individual portions. They are both practical and crowd pleasing.

CHILLED SPOONS

For a ceviche hors d'oeuvre, spoon out bite-size amounts of your favorite ceviche and place each filled spoon on a popcorn-lined tray. Guests can devour a mouthful of ceviche right off a chilled spoon.

CHILLED BOWL ON ICE

I like to display *mixtos* ceviches in large bowls atop mounds of crushed ice. Although you likely don't have the space at home for such an extravagant presentation, you can create something similar. Rest your serving bowl within a larger, decorative bowl filled with crushed ice or ice cubes.

about the recipes

You will notice as you work through the recipes in this book that the basic ceviche formula remains the same; it is simply layered with additional ingredients to make it more complex, often both in taste and in presentation. With all ceviches, whether you're making the simpler *tiraditos* or the more elaborate *mixtos*, there are two details that need special attention: ingredient quality and timing.

First, the importance of high-quality ingredients is especially true when preparing a simple ceviche, where the clean, unmasked flavors of each component must shine on their own without the help of many enhancements. The second key for successful ceviches is timing. Once again, the goal is to highlight your stellar ingredients. Being lax about marinating time can result in gummy, "over-cooked" seafood. Contrary to the practice of marinating a more complex protein like chicken or steak several hours or overnight, when it comes to marinating seafood, longer is not always better. The citrus acid can quickly break down the seafood's flesh past its prime state. But don't despair. It isn't difficult to get it right. Just pay close attention to the instructions

I've given and you'll be well on your way to your first, perfect ceviche.

I have divided the ceviche recipes in this book into two main chapters: *Tiraditos*, classic, simply prepared ceviches with minimal marinade and garnish ingredients, and *Mixtos*, mixtures of two or three types of seafood flavored with more intense ingredients. I hope the Side Dishes chapter will provide ample ideas for dishes to accompany the ceviches and encourage you to make an entire meal around them. Following these chapters, the Basics chapter will help you prepare some of the ingredients used in many of the recipes. I've also included a sources section to help you find local purveyors of the fresh seafood and some of the more exotic ingredients used in the recipes. Finally, the Glossary is a great place to consult for information when you encounter an unfamiliar ingredient or term.

Since I was a teenager, the thing I've loved most about cooking is the experimentation. There are so many lands to discover in this world, with so many new flavors, that a lifetime does not allow anyone to experience them all firsthand. But trying new recipes and innovative dishes at home is a great way to learn and a great way to travel to far-off lands straight from your own kitchen. May this book be a guide to ceviche—to lands already discovered as well as inspiration to conquer uncharted fresh tastes.

tiraditos

CHAPTER 1

You'll find my most straightforward ceviches in this chapter.

It offers two simple ceviches toward the beginning, one using sea bass, the other using grouper (pages 19 and 28), which stick primarily to the basic formula of citrus, salt, onions, herbs, and chiles. If you're preparing your first ceviche, start with these. *Tiraditos* typically include only one type of seafood and represent a rather minimalist approach to ceviche; a pure style where the main prize is the flavor of the fish itself rather than any marinade or garnish ingredients.

Roughly translated, *tira* means "throw" and *ditos* means "little bites," or "thrown-together little bites." This is an apt description of these simple, tossed preparations of any fish or seafood where the components of a classic ceviche—citrus, onion, and herbs—are used only to enhance the flavor of the fish rather than to add any strong characteristics of their own. The exciting part is that the following simple recipes will work with just about any seafood, so feel free to interchange bass with blue fish, salmon with scallops, or mackerel with merluza to match your mood.

During my travels through South America, I have spoken to many individuals who take pride in making ceviches, from home cooks along the Ecuadorian coast to the confident ceviche specialists who work magic at nothing more than roadside carts in Peruvian fishing villages. One especially inspirational friend of mine, Humberto Sato at Costanera 700, or "Coastal Restaurant 700," in Lima, Peru, embraces what I consider a true *tiradito* philosophy. He is a ceviche expert whose attention to quality ingredients approaches the religious. He is meticulous about choosing his suppliers, preaching that he only buys from certain fishermen whose practices he knows down to the force with which they pull a day's catch out of the water. As Humberto explains, if a fisherman pulls his catch out of the water too quickly, the fish may become stunned, making the flesh too tough for good ceviche.

Anyone I know who's traveling through Peru, I send to Humberto's restaurant. They might question my advice upon first approaching the factory-like building in Lima's rough San Miguel neighborhood. But as the elite, professional crowd there will attest, searching out Humberto's waterfront hideaway will result in an unforgettable afternoon meal.

When I visit Costanera 700, I love to listen to Humberto speak of his ceviche philosophies. He is of Japanese descent, but has lived in Lima for most of his life and considers himself Peruvian. An Eastern sense of discipline and respect for life are certainly a tremendous part of the ceviche tradition that Humberto has helped create.

Many Americans are unfamiliar with the fact that Peru, and many other Latin American countries, have large Asian populations. So it seems even more logical to draw comparisons between the different forms of sushi and sashimi and the different forms of ceviches. Of course, they are both raw-fish preparations. But philosophically, sashimi, or raw fish served virtually unadorned, is the Japanese counterpart of *tiraditos*. *Tiradito* ingredients are also often cut into thin slices, similar to sashimi, rather than chopped as in most of the *mixtos* ceviche recipes.

Walking along the waters of Central and South America provides unstoppable motivation for creating ceviche. Seeing the incredibly fresh fish, brought literally from water to table, is what really motivates me to make a simple *tiradito* ceviche. But you don't have to travel to far-off lands for inspiration. As Humberto suggests, know your supplier; one whom you can trust and who will answer your questions about procurement, freshness, and storage. As the recipes in this book attest, there are unlimited creative options for ceviche. But if you start with an exquisite piece of fish, these *tiraditos* are as good as it gets.

chilean sea bass with lemon oil

If you're a ceviche novice, this recipe is a very simple starting point. But the simple list of ingredients makes the flavor of the sea bass particularly important, so make sure to get a beautiful piece of fish. The lemon oil is a nice change from typical citrus juice because it adds a bit of richness to the fish's already silky texture. And if you cut the sea bass thinly, the end result is buttery and subtle. yield: 6 servings

1½ pounds Chilean sea bass fillet

MARINADE

Juice of 2 lemons

½ cup freshly squeezed lime juice

1 tablespoon salt

¼ cup coarsely chopped fresh cilantro

½ red onion, thinly sliced into half-moons

3 tablespoons Lemon Oil (page 115)

Set the sea bass on a baking sheet, cover with plastic wrap, and freeze for 1 to 2 hours, until very firm, but not frozen solid.

Once frozen, remove the sea bass from the freezer and, using a sharp knife, slice it crosswise very thin. Transfer to a nonreactive bowl and gently toss it with the marinade ingredients. Serve immediately.

corvina traditional

This recipe epitomizes what a great ceviche should be—crunchy, sweet, savory, tart, and rich all in one bite. Corvina, a type of sea bass, is the most widely used fish in South America for ceviche, and is very forgiving for the novice. Its firm, lean flesh holds up better to acid and is easy to either thinly slice or dice.

The combination of sweet potato and raw marinated fish is common in Peru, although there the potato might be roasted whole, sliced, and served fanned at the edge of a plate of ceviche similar to this crunchy, tart version. As you eat the marinated fish, pull away bites of sweet potato from the edge of the dish and enjoy both components at once. Don't be swayed to leave out the sweet potato garnish—you must try both the tart, firm fish and the potato in the same bite to really understand and savor how they work together. Leftover sweet potatoes make a great side dish for spicy foods.
yield: 6 servings

CANDIED SWEET POTATOES

$^1/_3$ pound peeled sweet potatoes, cut into $^1/_4$-inch dice

$^3/_4$ cup pure maple syrup

MARINADE

$^1/_2$ cup freshly squeezed lime juice

$^1/_4$ cup fresh celery juice

1 tablespoon salt

2 teaspoons aji amarillo paste (see page 121)

1 pound skinless corvina fillet, blood line removed and cut into $^1/_2$-inch dice

GARNISH

$^1/_4$ cup very finely diced celery

3 tablespoons finely diced red onion

3 tablespoons chopped fresh cilantro

$^1/_4$ cup whole cilantro leaves

To make the candied sweet potatoes, put the sweet potatoes, syrup, and $^3/_4$ cup water in a small saucepan and bring to a boil over medium-high heat. Reduce the heat to maintain a gentle simmer and cook until the potatoes are soft but still hold their shape, about 15 minutes.

Drain the potatoes, reserving the syrup, and let cool. Once the potatoes are at room temperature, put them back in the cooled syrup to store in the refrigerator until ready to use. Drain the potatoes well before using. You should have about 2 cups.

In a nonreactive bowl, whisk together the marinade ingredients until well combined. Add the corvina and toss to combine. Add the celery, red onion, and chopped cilantro and mix well.

Transfer the ceviche to individual glasses or a large shallow bowl. Place about 1 cup of the candied sweet potatoes on the sides of the glasses or bowl and top with the cilantro leaves. Serve immediately.

sweet shrimp and sea urchin tiradito

Delicious sweet shrimp from Maine have a relatively short season, from December through March, but they are worth tracking down for this pairing with creamy sea urchin roe. Small and delicate, coldwater Maine shrimp are usually sold shelled in small tubs and are mild and sweet enough to eat raw. They can be found along the New England coast in the winter at very reasonable prices, or ordered online frozen. These delicate shrimp are the only type of shrimp I enjoy raw in ceviches. Japanese ebi, which are flash frozen with tails on, are a good alternative.

Sea urchin roe, or uni, can be found in Japanese specialty markets and is sold on wooden trays. Its buttery rich texture is a perfect match with sweet shrimp and crunchy red pepper and onion.
yield: 6 servings

MARINADE

2 tablespoons freshly
squeezed lime juice

1 tablespoon Lemon Oil
(page 115)

2 teaspoons salt

9 ounces fresh sweet Maine
shrimp or fresh-frozen
Japanese ebi shrimp, cleaned
and halved lengthwise

PANCA PAINT

1 tablespoon extra virgin
olive oil

2 ounces yellow onion (about
1/2 small onion), chopped

2 cloves garlic, minced

1 tablespoon balsamic vinegar

1 tablespoon low-sodium
soy sauce

1 tablespoon honey

1 tablespoon ketchup

1 cup panca pepper paste
(see page 122)

2 ounces corn syrup

GARNISH

4 teaspoons very finely diced
red bell pepper

2 teaspoons finely diced red
onion

2 teaspoons finely minced
sun-dried tomato

2 teaspoons Crispy Ginger
(page 113)

1 teaspoon finely chopped
fresh chives

Lemon Oil for garnish
(page 115)

6 pieces (about 4 ounces)
sea urchin roe

In a nonreactive bowl, mix together the marinade ingredients until well combined. Add the shrimp and toss. Set aside.

To make the Panca Paint, heat the olive oil in a skillet over medium heat. Add the onion and garlic and cook until softened, about 5 minutes. Add the vinegar, soy sauce, honey, and ketchup and bring to a simmer. Cook briefly until combined and transfer the mixture to the jar of a blender with the panca paste and corn syrup. Purée the sauce until smooth; strain through a fine-mesh strainer, let cool completely, and transfer to an airtight container until ready to use. You should have about $1\frac{1}{2}$ cups. You'll only need about $\frac{1}{2}$ cup for this recipe; save the rest for another use. It will keep for a long time in the refrigerator.

To assemble the ceviche, using a clean wide paintbrush, brush a thick stripe of the Panca Paint down the center of two long rectangular platters. Divide the shrimp and arrange them facing the same direction, slightly overlapping, on top of each Panca Paint stripe. Sprinkle half of the red pepper, onion, tomato, ginger, and chives evenly over the shrimp on each plate. Drizzle the shrimp with lemon oil, and evenly place three pieces of urchin roe over the shrimp on each plate. Serve immediately.

four-citrus sea scallops with cucumber

Sea scallops, or conchitas, are slightly smaller than diver scallops. Strive to get the dry variety, or ones free of any water-collecting preservatives. I prefer to cook with scallops in their shells. Ideally, that's what you're looking for to prepare this recipe, but scallops out of their shell will work just fine. Conchitas cook quickly, so I've added four citrus juices to this dish; the combination has a lower acidity than lime alone and will actually slow down the "cooking" process. The Valencia orange and grapefruit also add a pleasant sweetness. yield: 6 servings

1½ pounds large sea scallops

Juice of 6 limes

1 tablespoon sea salt

1 pink grapefruit

Juice of 1 pink grapefruit

Juice of 1 Valencia orange

Juice of 5 lemons

1 cucumber, cut in half lengthwise, seeded, and thinly sliced into half-moons

3 green onions, thinly sliced

2 tablespoons finely chopped fresh chives

1 tablespoon finely chopped fresh cilantro

Set the scallops in a single layer on a parchment paper–lined baking sheet, cover with plastic wrap, and freeze for about 1 hour, until very firm, but not frozen solid.

Once frozen, remove the scallops from the freezer and slice crosswise into very thin rounds. In a nonreactive bowl, toss the sliced scallops in the lime juice and salt. Cover and refrigerate for 1 hour.

Peel the grapefruit by slicing off the top and bottom, setting it upright on a flat surface, and using a sharp knife to cut away the peel, white pith, and exterior membrane. Cut from top to bottom, following the curve of the fruit; don't cut too deeply into the flesh of the grapefruit. Holding the grapefruit in one hand, run a knife along one of the interior membranes toward the center of the fruit. Do this again along the neighboring membrane to remove each grapefruit section. Repeat until all sections are removed. Roughly chop the grapefruit sections and reserve.

Before serving, drain the scallops, discarding the lime juice. In a clean nonreactive bowl, blend the grapefruit, orange, and lemon juices and gently fold in the reserved grapefruit sections, the remaining ingredients, and the scallops.

halibut with lemon and coriander oil

It's no surprise that halibut works well in ceviche. It actually takes well to virtually any cooking method you can think of: roasting, baking, grilling, frying, you name it. It is for this reason that halibut is my single, favorite Northeastern fish. I just love its meaty, lean texture and versatility. West Coast halibut is also available (usually at a cheaper price), but it's inferior to an East Coast catch. I have to admit that the texture of halibut in ceviche is a bit on the chewy side, but it's still very worth using. In this recipe, the slight crunch from the crushed coriander seeds (the seeds of the cilantro plant) and their oil lend complementary flavor and just the right amount of pleasing texture. If I had to eat one fish for the rest of my life, it would be halibut. yield: 6 servings

---

1½ pounds skinless halibut fillet, cut crosswise into 3 pieces

½ cup freshly squeezed lime juice

1 tablespoon salt

CORIANDER OIL

3 tablespoons coriander seeds

1 tablespoon salt

3 tablespoons virgin olive oil

MARINADE

½ cup freshly squeezed lemon juice

2 tablespoons finely chopped Pickled Jalapeños (page 111)

2 tablespoons chopped fresh chives

½ cup coarsely chopped fresh cilantro

4 green onions, thinly sliced

½ red onion, thinly sliced into half-moons

Set the halibut on a baking sheet, cover with plastic wrap, and freeze for about 2 hours, until very firm, but not frozen solid.

Once frozen, remove the halibut from the freezer and slice it crosswise very thin. In a nonreactive bowl, combine the sliced halibut, the lime juice, and salt. Cover and refrigerate for 1½ hours.

To make the coriander oil, toast the coriander seeds in a dry sauté pan over high heat until they begin to pop, about 4 minutes. Crush the seeds and the salt with a mortar and pestle. In a small bowl, blend the crushed seeds with the oil and let rest at room temperature.

Before serving, gently toss the halibut and its lime juice with the marinade ingredients and drizzle with the coriander oil.

grouper with opal basil

Grouper is a Florida fish so, because of the years I spent in Miami, I naturally think of it when making ceviche. The practice of freezing a fish to allow for easy, thin slicing is particularly important with grouper since it can be very chewy when eaten raw. If you can find it, use black or red grouper, which are the least tough and the most flavorful varieties. yield: 6 servings

1½ pounds grouper fillet, skin removed

½ cup freshly squeezed lime juice

1 tablespoon salt

MARINADE

Juice of 2 lemons

3 shots Tabasco sauce, or to taste

¼ cup basil oil (see page 121)

2 jalapeños, split lengthwise, seeded, and finely diced

10 opal basil or other fresh basil leaves, cut into chiffonade

½ red onion, thinly sliced into half-moons

Set the grouper on a baking sheet, cover with plastic wrap, and freeze for at least 2 hours.

Once frozen, remove the grouper from the freezer and, using a sharp knife, slice it very thin. In a nonreactive bowl, toss the sliced grouper in the lime juice and salt. Cover and refrigerate for 1 hour. Before serving, add the marinade ingredients to the grouper and lime juice and gently toss.

salmon with mustard oil and scallions

Salmon is an excellent fish prepared almost any way: cured, smoked, cooked, or raw. Because of this, it is widely popular. If you are hesitant to make a ceviche with some of the more adventurous fish and seafood suggested in this book, this may be a good first ceviche to prepare. This recipe, my partner Tom Nally's favorite, is simple yet impressive for both ceviche experts and novices. yield: 6 servings

MARINADE

1/2 cup freshly squeezed lime juice

1 1/2 teaspoons salt

1/4 cup freshly squeezed orange juice

2 tablespoons mustard oil (see page 122)

3 jalapeños, seeds and membranes removed, finely diced

2 tablespoons chiffonade of mint leaves

1/4 cup coarsely chopped fresh cilantro

4 green onions, thinly sliced

2 tablespoons chopped fresh chives

1 1/2 pounds skinless salmon fillet, cut into 1/4-inch dice

1/2 red onion, thinly sliced into half-moons, for garnish

In a nonreactive bowl, blend all the marinade ingredients. Add the salmon and gently toss. Cover and refrigerate for 1 hour. Before serving, garnish with the red onion.

sweet and spicy mackerel

Most gastronomes speak disparagingly of mackerel, due to its reputation for having an overly fishy taste and its designation as the most popular canned fish in the world. But canned mackerel preserved in oil is no comparison to it in its freshly caught state, which offers a rich, buttery flavor and a beautiful, tasty skin that, if cleaned well, will add a nice chewiness to this ceviche. Mackerel's raw flavor is also far superior to its cooked flavor, accounting for its frequent use in sushi and sashimi.

When buying fresh mackerel, make sure it was caught within a day or two, since its quality deteriorates quickly from rapid fat oxidation. When you press your finger into the fish, if it feels firm and no indentation remains, make haste for your kitchen and get ready to change your opinion about mackerel. yield: 6 servings

---

1½ pounds mackerel fillet, skin removed (this is optional) and thinly sliced

1 cup freshly squeezed lime juice

1 tablespoon salt

MARINADE

1 tablespoon honey

¼ cup freshly squeezed lime juice

¼ cup freshly squeezed grapefruit juice

1 teaspoon aji amarillo paste (see page 121)

1 teaspoon panca pepper paste (see page 122)

GARNISH

3 green onions, all of the white and half of the green parts, thinly sliced

2 tablespoons chopped fresh chives

3 tablespoons coarsely chopped fresh cilantro

1 small red onion, thinly sliced

In a nonreactive bowl, gently toss the sliced mackerel in the lime juice and salt. Cover and refrigerate for 1 to 2 hours. When ready to serve, drain the mackerel, discarding the lime juice. In a clean nonreactive bowl, whisk together the marinade ingredients; add the mackerel and garnish ingredients and gently toss.

merluza with pickled jalapeños and lemon oil

Merluza is the true Chilean sea bass. It is a very lean, white, and clean-flavored fish that is actually prized more for its raw flavor than for its cooked flavor. After cooking, merluza's flesh becomes too soft and often falls apart, but in ceviche it holds up beautifully. If you can't find merluza, you can substitute whiting. yield: 6 servings

MARINADE

1/2 cup freshly squeezed lime juice

1 1/2 teaspoons salt

1/2 cup freshly squeezed lemon juice

1 tablespoon grated fresh ginger

2 tablespoons Pickled Jalapeños (page 111)

1/2 red onion, thinly sliced into half-moons

1 1/2 pounds merluza fillet, skin and bones removed and finely diced

GARNISH

1/3 cup coarsely chopped fresh cilantro

3 tablespoons Lemon Oil (page 115)

In a nonreactive bowl, blend all the marinade ingredients. Add the merluza and gently toss. Cover and refrigerate for 1 hour. Before serving, garnish with the cilantro and drizzle with the lemon oil.

choros à la chalaca

Although not considered ceviche, these colorful steamed mussels are another classic dish found in most restaurants across Peru. Fresh black mussels are steamed and served open faced, garnished with a spicy tomato sauce loaded with crisp vegetables. The creamy, sweet mussel meat; corn kernels and lima beans balance the acidic sauce and leave you craving more.

Fresh black mussels are very inexpensive and found in nearly every seafood counter in local supermarkets. If you can't find them, try frozen pre-cooked green-lipped mussels on the half shell. If steaming them yourself, be sure to save and freeze the extra cooking liquid to add to seafood soups or stews. yield: 6 servings

2 tablespoons extra virgin olive oil

2 shallots, peeled and sliced

1^1/$_2$ cups dry white wine

Juice of ^{1}/$_2$ lemon

6 sprigs flat-leaf parsley

6 sprigs thyme

Freshly ground black pepper

1^1/$_2$ pounds (about 36) Prince Edward Island mussels, brushed clean and debearded (see page 103 for cleaning instructions)

SAUCE

3 tablespoons freshly squeezed lime juice

1 heaping tablespoon tomato paste

2 teaspoons Tabasco sauce

GARNISH

5 ounces cooked fresh yellow corn kernels

4 ounces frozen lima beans, thawed

1 pint (about 7 ounces) grape tomatoes, thinly sliced

3 tablespoons diced red onion

3 tablespoons chopped fresh flat-leaf parsley

To cook the mussels, in a large, deep heavy saucepan with a lid, heat the olive oil over medium-high heat and add the shallots. Cook until just softened, about 3 minutes. Increase the heat to high, add the wine, lemon juice, herb sprigs, and pepper to taste and bring to a boil. Add the mussels, cover, and cook, shaking the pan frequently, until the mussels open, about 4 minutes. Strain the mussels, reserving the cooking liquid and shallots. Discard the herbs and any unopened mussels. When cool enough to handle, remove the outer shell from each mussel and discard, and with a sharp knife, cut the mussel away from the bottom shell to loosen it, but leave it in the shell.

To make the sauce, put ^{1}/$_2$ cup of the reserved mussel cooking liquid and all of the shallots in the jar of a blender with the lime juice, tomato paste, and Tabasco. Purée until very smooth.

Put the sauce in a large nonreactive bowl and add the corn, limas, tomatoes, onion, and parsley and toss well to combine. Line a large serving platter with crushed ice. Spoon some of the vegetable mixture onto each mussel on the half shell and arrange on the ice-lined platter. Serve immediately.

snapper with tangerine

There seem to be countless varieties of snapper; from living in Florida, I'm personally familiar with at least five or six. For this ceviche, it is ideal to use a smaller fish, one under 2 pounds, since the bigger the fish, the tougher the meat. Although most snappers do not vary much in flavor once they are cooked, the different snapper varieties can have a surprisingly wide range of tastes when raw. Genuine red snapper would be my first choice for this dish. If you can find it, culantro will offer a bit more pungency than its better-known relative cilantro, complementing the flavor of the fish and balancing the sweet tangerine. Look for culantro (sometimes called recao) in Latin or Caribbean markets.

yield: 6 servings

MARINADE

¹/₂ cup freshly squeezed lime juice

1 tablespoon salt

¹/₂ cup freshly squeezed tangerine juice

1 tablespoon finely chopped Pickled Jalapeños (page 111)

1 tablespoon finely chopped fresh oregano

6 fresh culantro leaves, julienned, or 1 tablespoon finely chopped fresh cilantro

3 shallots, thinly sliced

1¹/₂ pounds skinless snapper fillet, cut into ¹/₄-inch dice

2 tablespoons extra virgin olive oil

In a nonreactive bowl, whisk together all the marinade ingredients. Add the snapper and gently toss. Cover and refrigerate for 1 hour. When ready to serve, drizzle with olive oil.

whole sardines with fresh herbs and crème fraîche

I'm a huge fan of small fish such as anchovies, baiting, and, of course, sardines. Unfortunately, when many Americans think of sardines, they picture tiny fish drowned in oil, or some other saucy mixture, packed side by side in a small, flat can. But fresh sardines are a wonderful fish, nothing like their canned counterparts. Typically 5 to 6 inches in length, their flesh has a quite delicate flavor. If you can find them, sardines imported from Portugal have the best flavor.

Because of their small size, it is easiest to leave on the skin of sardines—it also imparts a great flavor. That said, remember that it is extremely important to wash the sardines very well, rinsing off all of their scales under cold water. Scoring the skin will allow the fish to more easily soak up the flavorful marinade. Don't marinate the sardines for any longer than 2 hours or they will become mushy and pasty. Just enjoy them as soon as they're done marinating, with a silky dollop of crème fraîche or sour cream. yield: 6 servings

4 pounds fresh sardines, cleaned, boned, and filleted

1 cup freshly squeezed lemon juice

2 tablespoons salt

10 cloves garlic, thinly sliced crosswise

6 shallots, thinly sliced

MARINADE

1/2 cup virgin olive oil

Leaves from 6 sprigs thyme

Leaves from 6 sprigs oregano

1/2 cup freshly squeezed lemon juice

1 tablespoon honey

1 tablespoon freshly ground black pepper

1 cup crème fraîche or sour cream for garnish

Lightly score each sardine crosswise on the skin side, three times per fillet. In a nonreactive bowl, combine the sardines, lemon juice, salt, garlic, and shallots. Cover and refrigerate for 2 hours. Before serving, drain the sardines, discarding the lime juice, garlic, and shallots. In a bowl, blend together the marinade ingredients. Add the sardines and gently toss. Garnish with crème fraîche.

bluefish with cream and horseradish

Since bluefish is typically very abundant, you will often find it smoked—the market's response to an oversupply of the fresh variety. So to be kind, I'd highly recommend taking some fresh bluefish off your fishmonger's hands. Once again, as with mackerel, the quality of bluefish deteriorates quickly once it's out of the water, so make certain you're getting a very fresh catch. The heavy cream used in this preparation can be omitted, but I love the richness it adds. It is akin to the tradition of mixing sour cream into the vinegar base of pickled herring. Here the flavor of the cream plays off the oiliness of the fish and the kick of horseradish. yield: 6 servings

1½ pounds skinless bluefish fillet, thinly sliced crosswise

½ cup freshly squeezed lime juice

1 tablespoon salt

MARINADE

1 teaspoon grated fresh horseradish

Juice of 2 Valencia oranges

6 cloves garlic, thinly sliced (preferably on a mandoline)

¼ cup heavy cream

1 teaspoon mayonnaise

1 tablespoon freshly ground black pepper

GARNISH

3 tablespoons julienned fresh flat-leaf parsley leaves

1 small red onion, thinly sliced

In a nonreactive bowl, gently toss the sliced bluefish in the lime juice and salt. Cover and refrigerate for 1 hour. When ready to serve, blend together the marinade ingredients in a clean nonreactive bowl and set aside. Drain the bluefish, discarding the lime juice, and gently toss it in the reserved marinade along with the garnish ingredients.

minted diver scallops with pummelo and bacon

The pummelo in this recipe is a nice change from the more traditional citrus fruits we're used to in the United States. Pummelos are similar to grapefruits, but with a thicker pith and skin. The pulp is also uniquely crisp (similar to the seeds of a pomegranate), and lends a distinctive texture to this recipe. If you must, you can substitute pink grapefruit, but the pummelo's milder sweetness and bright acidity are really a superior addition.

Diver scallops, or hand-harvested scallops, are not processed with any preservatives and will often have the coral-colored, half-moon of roe, or eggs, still attached—a rich addition you can dice right into the ceviche. The salty, smoked bacon adds another element of intensity and crunch. yield: 6 servings

1¹/₂ pounds diver scallops, about 15 pieces

MARINADE

¹/₂ cup freshly squeezed lime juice

1 tablespoon salt

¹/₂ cup freshly squeezed pummelo or pink grapefruit juice

¹/₂ cup chiffonade of fresh mint leaves

1 pummelo or two small pink grapefruits, peeled, sectioned, seeded, and cut into ¹/₂-inch dice

3 serrano chiles, thinly sliced crosswise

¹/₂ red onion, thinly sliced into half-moons

3 tablespoons chopped fresh chives

¹/₂ pound cooked smoked bacon, crumbled, for garnish

Set the scallops on a parchment paper–lined baking sheet, cover with plastic wrap, and freeze for about 1 hour, until very firm, but not frozen solid.

Once frozen, remove scallops from the freezer, 2 or 3 at a time, and slice each one into very thin rounds. In a nonreactive bowl, blend together the marinade ingredients. Gently toss the sliced scallops in the mixture. Refrigerate for about 2 hours or until the scallops have a whitish, more opaque appearance. Before serving, garnish with the bacon.

kingfish with orange juice and candied orange rind

As you might guess, kingfish, or king mackerel, is the largest mackerel variety, sometimes weighing up to 100 pounds (although most often they're between 10 and 20 pounds). Like other mackerels, it is best when eaten as fresh as possible. When I was growing up, my mother always used to make escabeche with kingfish steaks. She'd dust the fish in flour, fry it, and then marinate the steaks under vinegar in a heavy, clay casserole dish perched atop our refrigerator. The vinegar would have preserved the fish for a few days, but our family's batch never lasted longer than one day. The soft, oily flesh of kingfish has a strong flavor that stands up to the punch of vinegar or citrus used in ceviche and to strongly flavored accompaniments, like the garlic in this preparation. The candied orange rind is a perfect last touch, adding sweetness and a contrasting texture. yield: 6 servings

1¹/₂ pounds skinless kingfish fillet, cut into ¹/₄-inch dice

1 cup freshly squeezed lime juice

1 tablespoon salt

MARINADE

¹/₂ cup freshly squeezed orange juice

2 tablespoons panca pepper paste (see page 122)

4 cloves garlic, thinly sliced

1 small red bell pepper, seeded and cut into matchsticks

6 sprigs huacatay (see page 121) or mint

2 tablespoons thinly sliced jalapeños

4 shallots, thinly sliced

¹/₃ cup coarsely chopped fresh cilantro

2 tablespoons Candied Orange Rind (page 112) for garnish

In a nonreactive bowl, gently toss the kingfish in the lime juice and salt. Cover and refrigerate for about 1 hour. In a nonreactive bowl blend together the marinade ingredients and set aside. Drain the kingfish, discarding the lime juice, and gently toss it in the reserved marinade. Cover and refrigerate for 1 hour. Sprinkle with the candied rind before serving.

fiery escolar with panca pepper, tabasco, and horseradish

Just like fashion, foods can be trendy, falling in and out of favor in a matter of years or even months. The rise in popularity of escolar, or drum fish, is a perfect example of our fickle food preferences. More than a decade ago, escolar, a Gulf fish, was considered junk from the "bottom of the drum." But now it is cropping up on menus all across the country and even can be difficult to find due to its popularity with both chefs and consumers. I really enjoy escolar's mild white flesh in ceviche, and its high oil content plays off the spiciness of the panca pepper paste, Tabasco, and horseradish in this recipe. If you can't find escolar, substitute halibut, but the texture will suffer. yield: 6 servings

1¹/₂ pounds skinless escolar fillet

¹/₂ cup freshly squeezed lime juice

1 tablespoon salt

MARINADE

1 tablespoon Worcestershire sauce

¹/₂ cup freshly squeezed lime juice

¹/₄ cup freshly squeezed orange juice

1 tablespoon panca pepper paste (see page 122)

1 tablespoon Tabasco sauce

1 teaspoon prepared horseradish

3 plum tomatoes, seeded and diced

GARNISH

3 green onions, thinly sliced

¹/₂ red onion, thinly sliced into half-moons

¹/₄ cup coarsely chopped fresh cilantro

Cut the escolar into large rectangular pieces, each about 2 by 3 inches. Set the escolar pieces on a baking sheet, cover with plastic wrap, and freeze for 1 to 2 hours, until firm but not frozen solid.

Once frozen, remove the escolar from the freezer and slice it crosswise very thin. In a nonreactive bowl, combine the sliced escolar with the lime juice and salt. Cover and refrigerate for 1 to 2 hours.

When ready to serve, drain the escolar, discarding the lime juice. In a clean, nonreactive bowl blend together the marinade ingredients, and gently toss in the escolar and the garnish ingredients. Refrigerate for 1 hour before serving.

hamachi nikkei

During the late 1800s, and continuing into the mid-twentieth century, there was a steady stream of Japanese immigrants into Peru and Latin America, traveling there to work on farms. This influx of Japanese influence culminated in the country electing a Japanese president in 1990, Alberto Fujimori, who held office for ten years. In Latin America, the Japanese and their descendants, known as Nikkei, had a profound influence on local cultures and cuisines. This is very evident in ceviche and its many variations known today.

The Nikkei "movement" in cuisine is part Peruvian and part Japanese. My salute to that movement and its fascinating flavor and technique combinations is showcased here. I combine Japanese flavors like yuzu and togarashi (a spice blend of chile powders and dried pulverized orange peel) to create a visually beautiful and bright, balanced ceviche. yield: 6 servings

MARINADE

¼ cup yuzu juice
(see page 123)

¼ cup freshly squeezed
lime juice

2 tablespoons chiffonade of
Thai basil (see page 123)

Pinch of salt

Pinch of freshly ground
black pepper

12 ounces skinless hamachi,
very thinly sliced

SWEET SOY PAINT

1 cup kecap manis (see
page 122)

½ cup oyster sauce

GARNISH

1 teaspoon togarashi
(see page 123), or to taste

1 tablespoon nori furikake
(see page 122)

In a nonreactive bowl, whisk together the marinade ingredients. Add the hamachi and toss well.

To make the Sweet Soy Paint, whisk together the soy and oyster sauces in a small saucepan and bring to a simmer over medium-low heat. Simmer, stirring very frequently to prevent scorching, until the liquid is reduced by one-third, about 10 minutes. Immediately pour into a heatproof container and let cool completely before covering. You should have about 1 cup. You will only use about ¼ cup for this recipe; reserve the rest for another use.

To serve, use a clean 2½- or 3-inch-wide paintbrush to brush stripes of the soy paint along the outer long edges of a large rectangular platter, or serve the soy paint on the side in a small dipping bowl. Mound the hamachi evenly down the center to form a middle "stripe." Sprinkle the togarashi over the hamachi and the furikake on the plate around the fish. Serve immediately.

gingered toro tuna with soy and sesame

Toro, or tuna belly, approaches the status of a delicacy in Japan. And the fattier it is, the more it costs. There is a company in Spain that fishes tuna and raises it specifically to enhance the rich fattiness of the toro. The company nets the tuna, keeps it alive, and takes it to a farm to dine in ecstasy on a strict diet of sardines for a week or more. Some Japanese chefs will pay up to $500 a pound for high-quality toro tuna, making investments of up to $30,000 not out of the question.

With toro, it's really the texture—intense, velvety, and tender—that's important. In this ceviche, the honey and soy sauce accentuate the sweet, buttery flavors of the fish. You can substitute high-quality ahi tuna and the dish will be just as enjoyable. yield: 6 servings

1 pound tuna belly trimmed and cut into pieces about 2 by 3 inches

MARINADE

1 teaspoon honey

$1/2$ cup freshly squeezed lime juice

1 teaspoon grated fresh ginger

$1/2$ red onion, thinly sliced into half-moons

3 tablespoons Pickled Jalapeños (page 111)

$1/4$ cup soy sauce

$1/4$ cup coarsely chopped fresh cilantro

$1/4$ cup sesame seeds

Set the tuna on a baking sheet, cover with plastic wrap, and freeze it for 1 to 2 hours, until very firm.

Once frozen, remove the tuna from the freezer and slice it crosswise very thinly. In a nonreactive bowl, blend together the marinade ingredients. Add the tuna and gently toss. Serve immediately.

pompano with thai basil and candied orange rind

Pompano is a line-caught, warm-water fish that has a delicate flavor incomparable to any other oily fish. When cooked, its beautiful silver skin is valued almost as much as its flesh. Although the skin does not work well as an uncooked addition to this ceviche, try crisping it up by pan-frying it in olive oil and using it as a garnish.

The candied orange rind in this recipe tempers and enhances the oiliness of the fish. The crunchy, chewy bits of sweet rind are in keeping with the typical citrus flavors of ceviche and lend a surprising and unique texture to this dish. Make this for guests—the perfumed flavors and unique ingredients will bring smiles and add a sense of mystery. yield: 6 servings

1½ pounds skinless pompano fillet, thinly sliced diagonally

½ cup freshly squeezed lime juice

2 tablespoons sea salt

MARINADE

1 teaspoon aji amarillo paste (see page 121)

3 tablespoons virgin olive oil

¼ cup freshly squeezed lime juice

¼ cup freshly squeezed orange juice

GARNISH

¼ cup chiffonade of Thai basil (see page 123) or other fresh basil leaves

½ red onion, thinly sliced into half-moons

8 fresh chives, finely chopped

1 tablespoon Candied Orange Rind (page 112)

In a nonreactive bowl, gently toss the sliced pompano in the lime juice and salt. Cover and refrigerate for 1 to 2 hours. When ready to serve, blend together the marinade ingredients in a bowl and set aside. Drain the pompano, discarding the lime juice, and gently toss it in the reserved marinade along with the garnish ingredients.

sea urchin shots
with citrus soy sauce

In its natural state, the spherical, spine-covered body of the sea urchin might look like an ominous prospect for dinner. Resembling some kind of porcupine, urchins are actually siblings to the friendlier looking starfish. Yet, as with many unsightly culinary vessels, the sea urchin holds a jewel: its golden, silky roe, considered a delicacy in Mediterranean and South American regions as well as in Japan, where it's called uni.

Should you have the lucky opportunity to harvest roe straight from a fresh urchin, dislodging the roe is as easy as cutting a hole at the urchin's mouth, draining its fluid, and running your finger along the inside shell to dislodge the edibles. Most likely, you'll simply buy the roe at a sushi shop or Asian market. You'll notice the price, but it's worth it since you really can't get the rich, buttery taste of urchin roe in any other seafood. It's comparable to the richness of foie gras. As with anything this good, eat in moderation, as sea urchin's high iodine content makes excess consumption risky. This recipe's shot-glass presentation provides the perfect dose of heaven. yield: 6 servings

SAUCE

1/2 cup freshly squeezed lime juice

1/2 cup freshly squeezed orange juice

3 tablespoons soy sauce

1 teaspoon grated fresh ginger

1 teaspoon panca pepper paste (see page 122)

2 teaspoons honey

18 pieces (about 1 1/2 pounds) sea urchin roe

GARNISH

4 baby carrots, stemmed and thinly sliced

3 green onions, all the white and half the green parts, thinly sliced

3 shallots, thinly sliced

Baby cilantro sprigs or cilantro sprouts

When ready to serve, blend together all the sauce ingredients in a nonreactive bowl and set aside. Gently rinse the roe in cold water and drain. Place 3 pieces of roe in each of 6 shot glasses. Pour some of the sauce over the roe in each glass until just covered. Top each glass with a little of each garnish and eat in one mouthful, like a shot.

spiny lobster medallions with lime and horseradish

Once again, I've turned to a Florida resident for this simple ceviche: the spiny lobster. Eaten raw, these clawless creatures, commonly called rock lobster, or langouste *in French, offer an extra-sweet, rich flavor that doesn't compare to the raw Maine lobsters. Spiny lobsters get their name from the short spines that grow along the length of their tails and body and are recognizable by their colorfully spotted, orangy brown shells. The only edible part of the spiny lobster is the tail, and if you can't find the fresh variety look for frozen "rock lobster" tails at your local market. Fresh lobster are most easily found off the coasts of Florida or southern California and should not be expected to travel well to colder areas of the country during winter months.*

Keep in mind that when spiny lobsters are cooked, they loose their sweetness and become tough and rather stringy—that's why there is no marinating time in this recipe. yield: 6 servings

3 spiny lobster tails, shells split lengthwise and meat removed

1 orange

¹/₂ cup freshly squeezed lime juice

1¹/₂ teaspoons salt

1 teaspoon prepared horseradish

3 tablespoons Pickled Jalapeños (page 111)

¹/₄ cup coarsely chopped fresh cilantro

2 tablespoons virgin olive oil

Set the lobster meat on a baking sheet, cover with plastic wrap, and freeze for about 2 hours, until very firm, but not frozen solid. If you've purchased already frozen "rock lobster" tails, simply keep the tails frozen until you are ready to slice them.

Once the lobster meat is frozen, remove it from the freezer and slice it into very thin, round medallions and set it aside while you prepare the marinade. Peel the orange by slicing off the top and bottom, setting it upright on a flat surface, and use a sharp knife to cut away the peel, white pith, and exterior membrane. Cut from top to bottom following the curve of the fruit; don't cut too

deeply into the flesh of the orange. Holding the orange in one hand, run a knife along one of the interior membranes toward the center of the fruit. Do this again along the neighboring membrane to remove each orange section. Repeat until all sections are removed and squeeze the remaining fruit over a bowl to extract the juice. Roughly chop the orange sections and reserve them with the juice.

When ready to serve, blend together the lime juice, salt, and horseradish and gently toss in the lobster, chopped orange, 2 tablespoons of the reserved orange juice, the jalapeños, and cilantro. Drizzle the ceviche with the olive oil and serve immediately.

belon oysters with mustard oil and radish salad

Try to seek out the famed Belon oysters for this recipe. Although you can use any variety, the taste and size of Belons—indigenous to Brittany, France, but now raised in the United States—are worth the search. Nicknamed "les plates" after their shallow shells, Belons can measure up to 3½ inches in diameter and are known for their unique, slightly metallic flavor of brine and sweetness. Because of their celebrated flavor and tender bite, they are perfect for enjoying on the half shell or in this straight-forward ceviche preparation. yield: 6 servings

SALAD

6 red radishes, cut into matchsticks

½ of 1 medium daikon radish (see page 121), cut into matchsticks (about ½ cup)

3 shallots, thinly sliced

SAUCE

¼ cup mustard oil (see page 122)

½ cup freshly squeezed lime juice

1½ pounds (about 18) cold Belon oysters

Sea salt for sprinkling

As you prepare them, soak the salad ingredients in a bowl of ice water to keep them hydrated and crunchy. To make the sauce, blend together the mustard oil and lime juice. Drain the salad ingredients thoroughly and toss them in a bowl with the sauce. Cover and refrigerate while shucking the cold oysters, making sure to reserve their juices and shells (see page 99). Place each oyster back on a half shell, and spoon a bit of the reserved oyster juice over each shell. Sprinkle the oysters lightly with sea salt, and mound 1 heaping tablespoon of the salad on top of each. Serve immediately.

octopus à la oliva

Although not technically a ceviche, this impressive yet simple dish is included on nearly every menu in traditional ceviche restaurants across Peru; something akin to crab cakes here in the United States. Serving octopus may seem foreign, but if prepared properly, this visually stunning dish is sure to impress. Poaching the octopus properly is key; the water should just barely simmer so the octopus stays stationary while it cooks. Rapidly boiling water will jostle the tentacles and the skin can loosen or tear.

For this beautiful deep purple sauce classically served with octopus, be sure to use Alfonso olives and blend the sauce long enough to completely liquefy them so there are no black specks visible. If you have trouble finding Alfonso olives, use pitted kalamatas. yield: 8 servings

---

BLACK OLIVE SAUCE

⅓ cup vegetable oil

2 tablespoons extra virgin olive oil

1 large egg yolk

8 ounces pitted brine-cured Alfonso olives (see page 121)

4 jumbo octopus tentacles (about 4 ounces each), cooked (see page 100) and cooled

¼ medium red onion, very thinly sliced on a mandoline

Salt

8 fresh chives, cut into 1-inch segments

1 teaspoon Lemon Oil (page 115), plus more for drizzling

Put the vegetable and olive oils in the jar of a blender with the egg yolk. Add the olives and purée until the sauce is very smooth, is deep purple in color, and has no black specks, about 5 minutes. Set aside.

Slice the octopus on the bias into ¼-inch-thick slices and transfer the tentacles to a long platter, arranging them in their natural shape in long lines, leaving space between each one. Put the onion in a small bowl and soak in cold water for 5 to 10 minutes, until crisp and translucent. Drain and toss the onion with a pinch of salt, the chives, and 1 teaspoon Lemon Oil.

Drizzle more Lemon Oil over each tentacle and arrange the onion and chives mixture over the top. Spoon teaspoon-sized drops of Black Olive Sauce on the platter between the tentacles and serve immediately.

lemon-lime bay scallops with smoked paprika

Consumers are so used to seeing creamy white scallops piled on top of one another in a retail fish case, they often forget where the scallops were originally housed: in a shell much like that of an oyster or clam. They're really amazing, but unfortunately pretty difficult for the average consumer to find. Even if they are purchased already shucked, the light flavor of the scallops still produces wonderful ceviches.

I typically use strong flavors in ceviches for two reasons: to enliven a mildly flavored main ingredient and to stand up to a particularly strong one. This recipe is an example of the former, where jalapeños and smoked paprika pump up the impact of the delicate scallops. Smoked paprika is Spanish in origin and adds a surprise hint of spice and a depth of flavor incomparable to regular paprika. The red peppers used to make smoked paprika are dried and smoked before being ground into a powder. You can also try it sprinkled on other ceviches for color and a dash of smokiness. yield: 8 servings

---

3 green jalapeños, coarsely chopped including seeds

½ cup freshly squeezed lemon juice

½ cup freshly squeezed lime juice

2 pounds shelled bay scallops

6 plum tomatoes, seeded and diced small

¼ cup virgin olive oil

7 green onions, thinly sliced

¼ cup coarsely chopped fresh flat-leaf parsley

2 teaspoons salt

GARNISH

1 red onion, finely diced

1 tablespoon smoked or hot Hungarian paprika

In a blender, purée the jalapeños with the citrus juices and reserve. In a nonreactive bowl, gently toss the scallops with the tomatoes, olive oil, green onions, parsley, salt, and the puréed jalapeño mixture. Cover and refrigerate for 1 hour. Before serving, garnish the ceviche with red onion and sprinkle evenly with the smoked paprika.

salad-style conch with bell peppers and tomato

My very first experience with ceviche was eating conch ceviche, or conch salad, as they call it in Florida, after moving to Miami with my family at the age of 14.

I grew to love the Key West–inspired dish and quickly realized that it was a staple on most local restaurant menus. Back in Coconut Grove, the original Monty's Stone Crab and Seafood Restaurant had a great version of conch salad that always satisfied my cravings. At the time, I didn't realize I was actually eating a ceviche.

I've always been a big fan of this dish, partially because of its classic preparation and unadulterated taste and partially because it brings me back to my teenage years. I first served this ceviche as part of a "conch combo" at Yuca restaurant in Miami, paired with crispy conch fritters, a perfect accompaniment to the vibrant juices of the ceviche.

Although you may find other gastropods available in Italian or Chinese markets, such as scungilli (also known as whelk), or abalone, these are not conch. They are other species with very different taste profiles. You will probably not be able to find fresh conch, but you will easily find frozen conch in your grocer's freezer case. yield: 6 servings

1½ pounds conch meat, cleaned (see page 97) and cut into ½-inch dice

½ cup freshly squeezed lime juice

1 tablespoon salt

MARINADE

1 small red bell pepper, seeded and diced

1 small green bell pepper, seeded and diced

1 small red onion, diced

3 plum tomatoes, seeded and diced

1 tablespoon coarsely chopped fresh flat-leaf parsley

2 tablespoons coarsely chopped fresh cilantro

3 dashes Tabasco sauce

1 teaspoon salt

2 tablespoons coarsely chopped fresh cilantro for garnish

In a nonreactive bowl, toss together the conch, lime juice, and salt. Cover and refrigerate for at least 1 hour and up to 3 hours. When ready to serve, gently toss the conch with the marinade ingredients and garnish with the chopped cilantro.

mussels on the half shell with roasted red bell pepper

My favorite mussels, or choros, as they are called in Chile and Peru, are fresh from the cold waters of Prince Edward Island, Canada. Their clean diet makes them plump and meaty with a very consistent flavor and quality. The green-lipped variety that comes on the half shell in your grocer's freezer are actually a really great product that would work fine in this recipe.

This is a nice dish to serve as an appetizer to other ceviches—the antipasti of ceviche, if you will— or you can double the recipe to serve it as an entrée on its own. In Peru, you would probably order choros before any other ceviche. Classically, choros are prepared with a simple tomato salsa perched atop each one. Here, I've put a twist on the classic with the addition of huacatay, or Peruvian black mint, and roasted red bell peppers. If you want to impress guests, you can serve the mussels back in their shells. The presentation is a dramatic touch. yield: 8 servings

2 pounds (about 48) Prince Edward Island mussels, brushed clean and debearded (see page 103 for cleaning instructions)

1 cup clam juice or water

2 cloves garlic

2 jalapeños, roasted, peeled, seeded, and diced (see page 108)

¹/₂ cup freshly squeezed lime juice

¹/₂ cup freshly squeezed lemon juice

¹/₂ cup extra virgin olive oil

1 red bell pepper, roasted, peeled, seeded, and diced (see page 108)

2 tablespoons coarsely chopped huacatay (see page 121) or fresh mint leaves

2 shallots, thinly sliced

1 tablespoon salt

In a large, covered stockpot over medium-high heat, cook the mussels in the clam juice for 4 to 5 minutes, shaking the pot periodically (the movement will help the mussels open more quickly). Once the mussels are cooked, remove them from the pot with a slotted spoon, discarding the liquid in the pot. Remove the mussels from their shells and set them aside. Break the shells in half and reserve.

In a blender, purée the garlic, jalapeños, citrus juices, oil, and 2 tablespoons of the roasted red bell pepper and set aside. In a nonreactive bowl, gently toss the mussels with the remaining bell pepper, the huacatay, shallots, salt, and the puréed mixture. Cover and refrigerate for 1 hour. Serve the ceviche spooned back into the reserved mussel shells.

salmon bundles with pickled carrots, lime, and crunchy garlic

Though most of the recipes in this book would make great starters to any meal, these crunchy refreshing bundles make impressive party hors d'oeuvres. Serve them speared with a cocktail fork as a passed appetizer with drinks.

What makes this ceviche really special are the garnishes. The pickled carrots add great crunch and sweetness and the toasty garlic adds an earthy, nutty flavor to the salmon. Leftover pickled carrots are wonderful added to a sandwich or chopped in a salad. Toss the crunchy garlic nuggets with pasta or sprinkle on soup and drizzle the garlic oil over greens or roasted meats. yield: 6 servings

MARINADE

¼ cup freshly squeezed lime juice

2 tablespoons Lemon Oil (page 115)

2 green onions, thinly sliced

2 teaspoons salt

2 teaspoons chopped fresh chives

2 teaspoons chopped fresh cilantro

1 pound skinless salmon fillets, sliced against the grain into 12 thin rectangular pieces

2 tablespoons Garlic Oil (page 113)

3 cups Pickled Carrots (page 109)

1 tablespoon Crunchy Garlic (page 113)

In a nonreactive bowl, whisk together the marinade ingredients. Add the salmon slices, toss well, and let stand for 5 minutes. Remove the salmon and whisk the Garlic Oil into the marinade. Reserve the marinade.

Lay the salmon slices flat on a work surface. Place about ¼ cup of the Pickled Carrots on each salmon slice and roll up lengthwise to create a bundle; transfer them to a large serving platter. Spoon the marinade over the fish and sprinkle the top with Crunchy Garlic. Serve immediately.

mixtos

Now that you have a strong base of tiraditos *under your belt, it's time to toss in some stronger ethnic flavors and a generous helping of creativity.*

Mixtos, or "mixed" ceviches, are the next rung on the ceviche ladder and take the intricacies of ceviche just one step further. *Mixtos* include more than one type of seafood (typically two to three), have more intense sauce or marinade ingredients, and use more extravagant garnishes than the *tiraditos* variety. It is in Ecuador rather than Peru that you will likely find more *mixtos* ceviche preparations.

Each element of a *mixtos* ceviche is very important. Making a *mixtos* ceviche is like making a soup or a sauce: each ingredient adds flavor and texture, forming a complementary whole. It's really an art form—an art form of mixing flavors. Some people make the mistake of assuming that the more intricate *mixtos* ingredients are meant to mask the flavors of the fish. Not so! As with all ceviches, the key, once again, is incredibly fresh seafood combined with flavors that enhance rather than conceal.

And once again, the flavor-texture-color balancing act comes into play. Since *mixtos* often have a more liquid base than other ceviches, it is particularly important to balance their citrus acidity with other liquids, such as seafood stock.

Although when eating *tiraditos* ceviches you'll do fine with just a fork, you'll definitely want a spoon to scoop up the last drops of this chapter's *mixtos* creations.

ceviche verde of clams and sole

Necessity being the mother of invention, this ceviche was born out of a much-needed color contrast to my original palette of ceviches: black Peruvian Ceviche, white Honduran Ceviche with Coconut Milk, and red, tomato-based Ecuadorian Shrimp Ceviche. The combination of parsley and clams is actually a classic pairing, and the bright flavor of the verde sauce tastes fabulous in contrast to the saltiness of the clams. The verde sauce gets its color from spinach and parsley rather than chiles, as in salsa verde, so it's actually quite mild. When available, culantro, or "spiny coriander" as it's called in English, is a welcome garnish. Its leaves offer more punch than those of its close relative, cilantro.

Be aware that the lime juice in the ceviche will dull the chlorophyll in the sauce, taking away its vibrant green color within a few hours. For that reason, try to assemble this dish immediately before serving. yield: 6 servings

2 teaspoons virgin olive oil

12 littleneck clams, brushed clean

1 clove garlic, chopped

1/2 cup dry white wine

VERDE SAUCE

2 cups firmly packed fresh spinach, washed thoroughly

1/2 cup virgin olive oil

1 teaspoon salt

1 bunch green onions, trimmed

3 tablespoons coarsely chopped fresh flat-leaf parsley

GARNISH

1/3 pound boneless Serrano ham, cut into 1/4-inch dice

8 ounces sole fillet, cut into 1/4-inch dice

1 tablespoon sliced green onion

1 tablespoon chopped fresh chives

2 jalapeños, roasted, peeled, seeded, and chopped (page 108)

1 small red onion, diced

Juice of 3 lemons

Juice of 8 limes

6 fresh culantro or cilantro leaves, julienned, plus 2 tablespoons chopped culantro or cilantro for garnish

In a deep saucepan or stockpot, heat the olive oil over high heat and sauté the clams and garlic. When the garlic begins to brown, about 2 minutes, add the wine and cover. Cook for about 5 minutes more, or until the clams are open. Discard any clams that have not opened. Drain the clams, reserving the liquid for the verde sauce. Remove the clams from their shells and reserve for serving the ceviche.

In a blender, purée the verde sauce ingredients with enough liquid from the clams to make a bright-green, thick, smooth sauce.

In a nonreactive bowl, gently toss together the cooked clams, the garnish ingredients, and the verde sauce. Cover and refrigerate for 1 hour. Before serving, spoon the ceviche back into the reserved clam shells and garnish with the remaining chopped culantro.

amarillo ceviche mixto

This Peruvian ceviche offers a plethora of interesting textures: the meaty chew of octopus, the refreshing bite of shrimp, and the marshmallowy smoothness of bay scallops. It's all bathed in the electric yellow glow of a sauce made with Peru's most common chile pepper, the aji amarillo. You can find jarred aji amarillo paste at South American markets. The pepper imparts a distinct fruity quality to this dish, and the addition of turmeric and ginger enhances this fruitiness while toning down the pepper's heat. The variety of seafood in the following preparation, along with its exciting color, is certain to be a favorite on your table. yield: 6 servings

SAUCE

¹⁄₃ cup freshly squeezed lime juice

¹⁄₃ cup freshly squeezed lemon juice

1 tablespoon aji amarillo paste (see page 121)

1 tablespoon ground turmeric

¹⁄₄ cup clam juice

1 tablespoon grated fresh ginger

Pinch of salt

¹⁄₂ pound shrimp, peeled, deveined, and blanched (see page 102)

¹⁄₂ pound octopus, cooked (see page 100) and sliced crosswise into ¹⁄₈-inch slices

¹⁄₂ pound sautéed bay scallops (see page 98)

1 yellow tomato, seeded and diced

1 small yellow bell pepper, seeded and diced

1 tablespoon chopped fresh chives

2 tablespoons sliced green onions

1 tablespoon coarsely chopped fresh cilantro for garnish

Place all the sauce ingredients in a blender or food processor and purée until smooth. In a nonreactive bowl, mix together the sauce, shrimp, octopus, scallops, tomato, bell pepper, chives, and green onions. Cover and refrigerate for 1 hour. Before serving, garnish with the chopped cilantro.

paella ceviche

I love this ceviche. It is my interpretation of paella, the classic saffron-infused seafood and rice dish from Spain. The garnish of crunchy wasabi peas is a slight break with tradition, but their spice and bite are a welcome contrast and one akin to the Ecuadorian ceviche accompaniments of popcorn and corn nuts. The meaty texture of Prince Edward Island mussels are superior for this dish, but the green-lipped variety will also work. yield: 6 servings

6 cloves garlic, finely chopped

¼ cup extra virgin olive oil

18 Prince Edward Island mussels, brushed clean and debearded (see page 103 for cleaning instructions)

18 Manila clams, brushed clean

1 cup dry white wine

1 tablespoon saffron threads

½ tablespoon ground turmeric

SAUCE

1 tablespoon aji amarillo paste (see page 121)

¼ cup freshly squeezed lime juice

¼ cup freshly squeezed orange juice

1 teaspoon salt

SEAFOOD

½ pound cooked lobster meat, cut into ½-inch dice

½ pound shrimp, blanched (see page 102)

½ pound calamari ribbons (see page 106)

¼ pound bay scallops, blanched (see page 98)

GARNISH

4 jarred pequillo peppers, julienned (see page 122)

1 tablespoon coarsely chopped fresh flat-leaf parsley

¼ cup Lemon Oil (page 115)

½ red onion, thinly sliced into half-moons

½ cup crunchy wasabi peas

In a deep saucepan or stock pot over high heat, sauté the garlic in the olive oil for about 1 minute. Add the mussels, clams, and wine. Cover and cook for 4 to 5 minutes, shaking the pot periodically (the movement will help the shells open more quickly), until the mussels and clams have opened.

Transfer the mussels and clams from the pot to a large bowl, leaving the liquid in the pan and discarding any mussels and clams that have not opened. Cover the mussels and clams and refrigerate until ready to assemble the dish. Stir the saffron threads and turmeric into the mussel liquid. Over very high heat, reduce the liquid by half, to approximately ½ cup; let cool.

In a blender, combine the ½ cup mussel liquid with the sauce ingredients and blend until smooth. In a bowl, mix the seafood ingredients, including the cooked mussels and clams, with the blended sauce. Fold in all the garnishes except the onion and peas, and refrigerate for 20 minutes. To assemble each portion, arrange 3 mussels and 3 clams around the perimeter of a round plate, spoon ceviche into the center, and drizzle the mussels and clams with some of the ceviche juices. Garnish with the onion and peas.

ecuadorian shrimp

This dish was inspired by a trip I made to Ecuador. A friend of mine, Humberto Sato, took me on a tour of the country. In the city of Salinas, we visited a restaurant called La Lojanita, that served only ceviches. There were close to twenty different ceviches on the menu, ranging from giant clam to octopus, mussels, and oysters. During our stay in Salinas, we must have tried all of them, and the one that impressed me the most was a tomato-based shrimp ceviche. This recipe echoes both that ceviche and the Ecuadorian custom of placing bowls of popcorn and corn nuts on the table when serving ceviches.
yield: 4 servings

SAUCE

1 large tomato, roasted, peeled, seeded, and chopped

2 jalapeños, roasted, peeled, seeded, and chopped

1 red bell pepper, roasted, peeled, seeded, and chopped

1/2 onion, roasted, peeled, and chopped

3/4 cup freshly squeezed lime juice

1/2 cup freshly squeezed orange juice

1/4 cup canned tomato juice

1 tablespoon sugar

3 shots Tabasco sauce, or to taste

Pinch of salt

1 pound extra-large shrimp (16 to 20), blanched (see page 102)

1 small red onion, thinly sliced

2 tablespoons chopped fresh chives

2 tablespoons sliced green onions

1/4 cup coarsely chopped fresh cilantro

1/2 cup freshly popped plain, unsalted popcorn for garnish

1/2 cup unsalted corn nuts for garnish

Roast, peel, seed, and chop the tomato, jalapeños, bell pepper, and onion (see page 108). In a blender, purée the sauce ingredients until smooth and refrigerate until ready to use. Before serving, in a nonreactive bowl, toss the shrimp with the sauce, red onion, chives, green onions, and cilantro. Garnish with popcorn and corn nuts.

honduran fire and ice lobster

I served a similar tuna ceviche at Patria for many years, a spicy yet ice-cold mixture (hence the name) that was scooped into a coconut shell and dramatically garnished with fried plantains. Since then, I've seen the presentation imitated in numerous other restaurants. Here I've added lobster stock and fresh lobster meat. The coconut milk is a reminder of this dish's Honduran heritage; the country grows and exports coconuts and is also famous for its ceviches.

Despite the heat present in this dish from the ginger and jalapeño, it is refreshing and its dramatic presentation in a coconut shell is a guaranteed crowd-pleaser. The bell pepper, watercress, and shaved coconut garnishes can be arranged around the perimeter of the coconut shell for color and effect. Of course, the presentation is just as beautiful if you serve the ceviche in a deep bowl and decorate the bowl's perimeter with the garnish ingredients. yield: 8 servings

4 fresh coconuts (optional)

1 jalapeño, chopped, with seeds

2 tablespoons chopped fresh ginger

$1/4$ cup Lobster Stock (page 104)

1 tablespoon sugar

$1/2$ cup freshly squeezed lime juice

1 can (14 ounces) unsweetened coconut milk

$1^1/2$ pounds cooked Maine lobster meat, cut into $1/4$-inch dice

$1/2$ red onion, thinly sliced into half-moons

$1/4$ cup shaved coconut

2 tablespoons sliced green onions

1 tablespoon finely chopped fresh chives

3 tablespoons finely chopped fresh cilantro leaves

GARNISH

1 batch Fried Plantains (page 107)

$1/2$ cup seeded and diced red bell pepper

1 bunch watercress, leaves only

2 cups shaved coconut

Lay out a damp kitchen towel on a stable work surface. Using the back of a heavy knife, whack a coconut along its circumference while rolling and rotating it along the toweled surface until it starts to split open. To catch the water, give the coconut its last whack in a heavy bowl. Once open, pat the insides of the coconuts dry, cover, and refrigerate.

Place the jalapeño, ginger, lobster stock, sugar, lime juice, and coconut milk in a blender and purée until smooth. In a nonreactive bowl, toss the lobster with the puréed mixture. Sprinkle with the red onion, the $1/4$ cup shaved coconut, green onions, chives, and cilantro. Place the mixture in the coconut halves, dividing equally, and garnish with plantain slices, bell pepper, watercress leaves, and the 2 cups shaved coconut.

peruvian black ceviche with squid ink and mixed seafood

This ceviche was inspired by a black clam ceviche I tried in Peru. When I returned to the United States, I couldn't find a source for black clams, so I came up with the idea of adding squid ink (available at Italian markets or specialty food stores) to the ceviche. Sometimes I like to add some minced Scotch bonnet chiles for a spicy effect. This dish makes a delicious, low-fat summer appetizer. yield: 10 servings

2 1/2 pounds mixed seafood (clams, mussels, scallops, calamari, octopus, fish)

4 cups clam juice, fish stock, mussel stock (page 103), or water

SAUCE

2 jalapeños, roasted, peeled, and chopped with seeds (see page 108)

1 red bell pepper, roasted, peeled, seeded, and chopped (see page 108)

1/2 onion, coarsely chopped

2 cloves garlic, chopped

2 tablespoons chopped celery

2 teaspoons squid ink (optional)

1 1/2 cups freshly squeezed lime juice

1/2 cup freshly squeezed orange juice

2 teaspoons salt

3 tablespoons extra virgin olive oil

GARNISH

1/2 red onion, thinly sliced into half-moons

2 tablespoons sliced green onion

2 tablespoons finely chopped fresh chives

3 tablespoons coarsely chopped fresh cilantro

1/4 cup diced tomato

Clean and prepare each seafood appropriately: Brush clean the clams and mussels, and debeard the mussels. Rinse the calamari and octopus; remove the skin and bones from the fish; and chop the calamari, octopus, and fish into bite-size pieces. For the scallops, calamari, octopus and fish, bring 3 cups of the clam juice to a boil in a large saucepan over high heat. Add the seafood, except for the clams and mussels, and blanch for about 1 minute, until slightly opaque. Drain and place in a large bowl. For the clams and mussels, bring the remaining 1 cup clam juice to a boil in a medium, covered stockpot. Add the mussels and clams and cook for 4 to 5 minutes shaking the pot periodically (the move-ment will help the shells open more quickly), until the clams and mussels have opened. Using a slotted spoon, transfer the clams and mussels (discarding any that failed to open) to the bowl of blanched seafood.

To make the sauce, place the jalapeños, bell pepper, onion, garlic, celery, squid ink, citrus juices, and salt in a blender or food processor and purée until smooth. With the motor running, slowly add the olive oil. Pour the sauce over the mixed seafood and toss gently. Refrigerate the ceviche for at least 2 hours. Just before serving, toss the garnish ingredients with the ceviche and transfer to serving plates.

campache mixto

Adapted from a Mexican-style ceviche, this combination of shellfish and octopus makes a vibrant presentation for a dinner party. A Mexican preparation might utilize ancho or chipotle chiles rather than the tangy spice of panca pepper, but the recipe always includes octopus and oysters and is served with sliced avocado.

The key to perfectly marinated oysters is leaving them in the lime juice until the edges just begin to curl, which will add a firmer texture. Once the sauce and fish are combined, the mixture holds well and can be easily made ahead. As always, slice the avocados just before serving. yield: 6 servings

SAUCE

2 tablespoons vegetable oil

1 tablespoon chopped fresh garlic

Salt

1/2 cup clam juice

6 tablespoons ketchup

1/4 cup panca pepper paste (see page 122)

1/4 cup tomato juice

12 freshly shucked oysters, drained

1/4 cup freshly squeezed lime juice

2 teaspoons salt

8 ounces blanched large shrimp (see page 102), halved lengthwise

2 tentacles cooked jumbo octopus (see page 100), about 8 ounces, thinly sliced

GARNISH

1 tablespoon diced red onion

1 tablespoon chopped fresh chives

1 tablespoon chopped fresh cilantro, plus whole leaves for garnish

Tabasco sauce, to taste

Salt

2 ripe avocados, peeled, pitted, and thinly sliced lengthwise

Freshly squeezed lemon juice for garnish

Extra virgin olive oil for garnish

To make the sauce, heat the oil over medium-high heat. Add the garlic and a pinch of salt and cook, stirring, until the garlic just begins to brown, 2 to 3 minutes. Carefully add the clam juice and simmer until the liquid is reduced by half, 2 to 3 minutes. Remove from the heat, whisk in the ketchup, pepper paste, and tomato juice, and let cool completely before chilling in the refrigerator.

In a nonreactive bowl, stir together the oysters, lime juice, and salt and let stand until the edges of the oysters begin to curl, about 5 minutes. Strain half the liquid from the oysters and discard. Add the shrimp, octopus, red onion, chives, chopped cilantro, Tabasco, and the chilled sauce and stir well. Taste the mixture and season with salt and additional Tabasco if desired.

To serve, fan the avocado slices evenly around the edge of a large round plate. Mound the seafood mixture in the center of the plate and drizzle the avocado with lemon juice, olive oil, and salt. Garnish the plate with cilantro and serve immediately.

chino latino black bass
with dried scallops

The dried scallops I call for in this recipe are not dry sea scallops, or scallops that have been plumped up with water and the preservative tripolyphosphate, but hard, air-dried scallops. I was introduced to the virtues of air-dried scallops by the Hawaiian chef Roy Yamaguchi. The first time I met him he was chewing on them, explaining that when he was a kid growing up in Japan, the salty, chewy snacks were eaten along with a can of soda—the equivalent of American potato chips.

You'll find a wide range of prices for air-dried scallops, which are often stored in glass jars at Asian markets, the larger varieties commanding higher prices. Air-dried scallops, or kan pooi or koong yi chi in Chinese, come from China as well as Japan and provide a nice textural addition to ceviche, their sweet, pungent flavor balancing perfectly with salty soy sauce. yield: 6 servings

MARINADE

1/4 cup freshly squeezed orange juice

1/4 cup soy sauce

2 tablespoons honey

2 tablespoons grated fresh ginger

1 teaspoon crushed red pepper flakes

1 1/2 pounds skinless black sea bass fillet (or striped bass), finely diced

3 ounces air-dried scallops, finely diced

4 green onions, thinly sliced diagonally

GARNISH

1/4 cup coarsely chopped fresh cilantro

1 tablespoon black sesame seeds

1/2 red onion, thinly sliced into half-moons

Sesame oil for drizzling (optional)

In a nonreactive bowl, blend together all the marinade ingredients. Add the bass and scallops and gently toss. Cover and refrigerate for 2 hours. Before serving, toss the bass and scallop mixture with the green onions. Garnish with the cilantro, sesame seeds, and red onion, and drizzle with sesame oil.

thai bigeye tuna and squid with coconut water

This is one of my favorite ceviches because each ingredient really perks up the natural flavor of the tuna; fresh coconut water, pungent garlic, sharp chiles, Thai basil, and earthy galanga add to the aroma. The consistency is not creamy, as you might expect from the coconut water, but instead very light and clean. Coconut water is greatly valued in Thai cooking and very different from coconut milk, which would easily overpower this dish. It actually adds a perfumy, even grassy quality to the marinade. You can find frozen coconut water in Asian markets.

Make sure you purchase bigeye tuna, also known as ahi. It is the deep, red variety you'll often see prepared as sushi or sashimi. Don't purchase yellowfin, which is whiter in color. Also, eat this ceviche as soon as you make it, since the clean flavors will quickly dissipate if it is over-marinated.
yield: 6 servings

1 pound center-cut boneless bigeye tuna

1 cup coconut water (see page 121)

¹⁄₂ cup freshly squeezed lime juice

¹⁄₄ cup Garlic Oil (page 113)

GARNISH

6 red Thai chiles (see page 123), finely chopped

3 green onions, all of the white and half of the green parts, thinly sliced

2 tablespoons chopped fresh chives

¹⁄₄ cup coarsely chopped fresh cilantro

¹⁄₄ cup chiffonade of Thai basil (see page 123) or other fresh basil leaves

2 kaffir lime leaves (see page 122), finely chopped

1 tablespoon grated galanga (see page 121)

¹⁄₂ red onion, thinly sliced into half-moons

¹⁄₂ pound calamari ribbons (see page 106) for garnish

Set the tuna on a baking sheet, cover with plastic wrap, and freeze it for at least 1 hour, until very firm, but not frozen solid.

Once frozen, remove the tuna from the freezer and cut it into ¹⁄₄-inch dice. In a nonreactive bowl, blend together the coconut water, lime juice, and Garlic Oil. Add the tuna and the garnish ingredients and gently toss. Scatter the calamari ribbons on top of the ceviche before serving.

japanese salmon with wasabi and shiso

Don't worry if you can't find or do not want to purchase each and every ingredient in this recipe. Some are a bit difficult to locate, although most are available in Asian markets or through the retailers listed in the sources section, page 117. The idea here is to create a dish that is inspired by Japanese flavors, so one or two missing components won't make or break the finished product.

Given that, if you're going to search, the most important ingredient to find is shiso—often called Japanese basil or perilla (see page 123). It adds a fresh, herbal note, similar to the Peruvian huacatay, or black mint, used in some of my other recipes, but with its own distinctively Japanese flavor. Look for the fresh variety during summer and fall. The bonito flakes, or dried fish shavings, are more about texture, and are less critical. yield: 6 servings

MARINADE

¹/₂ cup freshly squeezed lime juice

1 teaspoon salt

¹/₄ cup ponzu (see page 122)

¹/₄ cup soy sauce

1 tablespoon wasabi powder (see page 123)

¹/₂ red onion, thinly sliced into half-moons

10 leaves shiso, julienned

1 pound skinless salmon fillet, finely diced

¹/₄ cup bonito flakes (see page 121) for garnish

¹/₂ pound smoked eel, sliced crosswise into 6 equal slices for garnish

In a nonreactive bowl, blend together all the marinade ingredients. Add the salmon and gently toss. Cover and refrigerate for about 1 hour. Before serving, garnish with the bonito flakes and eel.

indian mussels with pineapple juice and curry

When you taste this ceviche, you'll instantly understand why pineapple and curry are two classically married flavors—the sweetness of the pineapple cuts through the complex, mellow heat of the curry. Feel free to adjust the spiciness to your taste by adding more or less curry powder. The flavors here will be even more impressive if you make the investment in a high-quality, jumbo-lump crabmeat with little or no cartilage. As always, I'd recommend Prince Edward Island mussels, if you can find them. Most likely, they will already be debearded by your fishmonger. yield: 6 servings

3 cloves garlic, finely diced

¼ cup extra virgin olive oil

36 Prince Edward Island mussels, brushed clean and debearded (see page 103 for cleaning instructions)

1½ cups clam juice

MARINADE

¾ cup freshly squeezed lime juice

½ cup pineapple juice

1 tablespoon curry powder

2 teaspoons grated fresh ginger

1 teaspoon salt

GARNISH

1 pound jumbo-lump crabmeat

3 plum tomatoes, seeded and diced

4 green onions, all of the white and half of the green parts, thinly sliced

2 tablespoons chopped fresh chives

¼ cup coarsely chopped fresh cilantro

½ red onion, thinly sliced into half-moons

In a large stockpot over medium-high heat, sauté the garlic in the olive oil for 1 minute. Add the mussels and the clam juice. Cover and let cook for 4 to 5 minutes, shaking the pot periodically (the movement will help the mussels open more quickly). Once the mussels have opened, remove them from the pot with a slotted spoon, leaving the liquid behind. Over medium-high heat, reduce the liquid by half, to about ¾ cup; let cool.

To make the marinade, in a bowl whisk the mussel liquid with the lime juice, pineapple juice, curry powder, ginger, and salt and set aside. Pick the mussels out of their shells and discard the shells, including any that have not opened. In a bowl, gently toss the mussels and the garnish ingredients with the reserved marinade. Serve chilled.

smoky maine shrimp with tangerine

Often referred to as "sweet shrimp," Maine shrimp have a very short season, typically only from December through March. They are small, often sold with their heads still on, and work just beautifully in raw preparations like ceviche. Be careful not to overcook the shrimp. It only takes a matter of seconds. And if you can't find Maine shrimp, a larger variety will work just fine sliced lengthwise down the vein. You can omit the fish sauce if you don't care for its flavor, although it really draws out the delicate taste of the shrimp. The chipotles in this ceviche add a smoky spiciness that complements the sharp sweetness of the tangerine. yield: 6 servings

1½ pounds Maine shrimp, heads and shells removed

SAUCE

2 canned chipotle peppers in adobo, roughly chopped

¾ cup freshly squeezed lime juice

½ cup freshly squeezed tangerine juice

2 teaspoons salt

1 tablespoon fish sauce

3 tablespoons ketchup

GARNISH

4 plum tomatoes, seeded and diced

4 green onions, thinly sliced

2 tablespoons chopped fresh chives

⅓ cup coarsely chopped fresh cilantro

½ red onion, thinly sliced into half-moons

Bring 1 gallon of salted water to a boil in a large pot. In 2 small batches, cook the shrimp for about 30 seconds, or just until they are opaque. Scoop the cooked shrimp out with a strainer and allow the water to return to a boil before cooking the next batch. As the shrimp are cooked, drain them, lay them on a baking sheet, and allow them to cool in the refrigerator.

To make the sauce, combine the chipotle peppers, citrus juices, salt, fish sauce, and ketchup in a blender and purée until smooth. In a nonreactive bowl, gently toss the cooled shrimp with the sauce and the garnish ingredients and marinate for 2 hours before serving.

tuna watermelon ceviche

I have served a version of this modern spin on ceviche for many years in my restaurants and it con-tinually gets the best response from my hungry customers. This could be the quintessential combina-tion, encompassing all the characteristics that make ceviche so irresistible. This recipe is sweet, spicy, tart, crunchy, soft, and cooling all in one bite.

The unexpected sweet softness of the candied kumquats and the refreshing bite of watermelon with firm deep-red tuna make this a perfect recipe for a party. It can be made ahead and holds well, unlike many other more acidic ceviches. For a dramatic presentation at your next gathering, serve it in a hollowed frozen baby watermelon shell. yield: 6 servings

MARINADE

5 tablespoons freshly squeezed lime juice

3 tablespoons sambal oelek (see page 122)

2 tablespoons Lemon Oil (page 115)

1½ tablespoons yuzu juice (see page 123)

2 teaspoons salt

GARNISH

1 tablespoon chiffonade of fresh basil

1 tablespoon finely chopped fresh chives

1 tablespoon chopped fresh cilantro

1 tablespoon finely chopped fresh tarragon

1 tablespoon finely chopped red onion

1 pound center-cut boneless ahi tuna, cut into ¼-inch dice

9 ounces cubed (¼-inch) fresh ripe seedless watermelon

2 tablespoons candied kumquats in syrup (see page 112)

In a large nonreactive bowl, whisk together the marinade ingredients. Gently fold in the garnish ingredients, the tuna, watermelon, and kumquats, and serve immediately.

beef tenderloin
with citrus-truffle mayonnaise

Here is where ceviche and carpaccio meet. In my version of the latter, I keep most of the elements of the classic Italian dish, which consists of thinly sliced, raw beef drizzled with freshly squeezed lemon juice or a mayonnaise-based sauce and garnished with capers and onions. Here, the earthy sweetness of the beef's Dried Mushroom–Adobo Rub, the citrus and truffle undertones of the sauce, and the fresh garnishes all add a Latin twist to the dish. Freezing the meat and using a good, sharp knife will ensure thin slices and an elegant and impressive presentation for you and your guests. yield: 6 servings

1½ pounds beef tenderloin, trimmed of silver skin

¼ cup Dried Mushroom–Adobo Rub (page 114)

2 tablespoons extra virgin olive oil

SAUCE

¼ cup freshly squeezed lime juice

¼ cup freshly squeezed orange juice

2 tablespoons mayonnaise

1 tablespoon black truffle oil (see page 121)

1 teaspoon salt

GARNISH

2 avocados, peeled, pitted, and thinly sliced

Freshly ground black pepper

2 tablespoons chopped fresh chives

4 green onions, thinly sliced

½ cup coarsely chopped fresh cilantro

1 red onion, halved and thinly sliced into half-moons

In a shallow dish, rub the beef tenderloin with the Dried Mushroom–Adobo Rub, cover, and refrigerate overnight. In a large sauté pan over very high heat, sear the tenderloin in the olive oil, 1 to 2 minutes on each side, until the outside is dark and charred. Let cool; cover and refrigerate until ready to freeze (as long as overnight). Freeze the tenderloin for at least 2 hours, until very firm, but not frozen solid.

Once frozen, remove the tenderloin from the freezer and slice it crosswise into very thin rounds. Spread the tenderloin slices on wax paper, cover, and refrigerate.

To make the sauce, whisk together the citrus juices, mayonnaise, truffle oil, and salt in a bowl. Cover and refrigerate. Before serving, arrange the tenderloin slices in overlapping circles on a serving plate. Arrange the avocado slices on top of the beef and sprinkle with the pepper, chives, green onions, cilantro, and red onion. Drizzle with the sauce.

lemon-orange mushrooms with truffle oil

With all this talk about ceviche's typical seafood base, you might be surprised to hear that mushroom ceviche is actually a classic Peruvian recipe. When I was a child, a Peruvian friend of my father's brought over a mushroom ceviche for my family to taste. That was one of my very first ceviche experiences and the memory of it is still vivid in my mind. But even though I loved the flavor, the experience actually distorted my impression of ceviche and it took years before I realized that ceviche was primarily a seafood preparation. Still, the standard ceviche elements present in this recipe add just as much life to mushrooms as they do to fish. Don't waste your money on anything besides button mushrooms for this dish. The deep, rich flavors of any other wild variety wouldn't meld well with the strength of the citrus, pickled jalapeños, and truffle oil. The button mushrooms provide a perfect clean and delicate flavor backdrop. yield: 6 servings

1½ pounds small, white button mushrooms, stems removed flush with caps

⅓ cup virgin olive oil

1 teaspoon kosher salt

1 cup freshly squeezed lemon juice

½ cup freshly squeezed orange juice

GARNISH

3 tablespoons Pickled Jalapeños (page 111), finely chopped

⅓ cup coarsely chopped fresh cilantro

4 green onions, thinly sliced

½ red onion, thinly sliced into half-moons

1 small red bell pepper, seeded and finely diced

3 tablespoons finely chopped fresh chives

3 tablespoons black truffle oil (see page 121)

Wipe the mushroom caps with a damp cloth to remove all dirt. In a nonreactive bowl, toss the mushroom caps with the olive oil and salt and let sit for about 10 minutes. Stir in the lemon and orange juices; cover and refrigerate for 2 hours. Before serving, fold in the garnish ingredients. Drizzle the truffle oil over the ceviche.

peruvian orange duck

Duck is another traditional Peruvian ceviche foundation that elicits surprise. Here, the duck is actually marinated first, then baked, before being dressed for its final presentation. The concept of using citrus in a ceviche to tone down the fattiness of a particular fish works just as well here with the rich duck meat. Reserving the duck juices from the baking pan is probably the most important step in this recipe. The liquid is transformed, with the addition of lime juice, onion, and cilantro, into a very unique sauce with deep, multilayered flavors. You'll notice that the marinade ingredients include duck's classic orange accompaniment, but the aji amarillo and panca pepper pastes veer away from tradition and really enliven this dish. yield: 6 servings

MARINADE

1 cup freshly squeezed orange juice

2 tablespoons aji amarillo paste (see page 121)

1 tablespoon panca pepper paste (see page 122)

4 cloves garlic, finely chopped

2 dried bay leaves

1 tablespoon dried oregano

1 tablespoon salt

Grated zest of 1 orange

2 tablespoons whole allspice berries

4 duck legs (about ½ pound each), skin removed, each one cut into 3 pieces

SAUCE

½ cup freshly squeezed lime juice

1 red onion, halved and thinly sliced

⅓ cup coarsely chopped fresh cilantro

3 tablespoons chopped fresh chives

1 tablespoon freshly ground black pepper

Pinch of salt

In a large bowl, mix together the marinade ingredients. Add the duck pieces, stir to coat, and let marinate, covered in the refrigerator, for about 6 hours.

Preheat the oven to 350°F. Remove the duck from the marinade, discarding the marinade, and place the pieces in a baking dish. Cover with foil and bake until tender, 1 to 1½ hours. Remove from the oven and let cool completely, about 1 hour. When cool, strain the liquid from the pan into a small bowl. In a blender, combine the sauce ingredients with the reserved liquid and blend until smooth. Place the duck pieces on a serving platter, cover with the sauce, and serve.

side dishes

papas huancaina

The Huancayo Indians of Peru created Huancaina—a creamy, classic sauce that gets its vibrant yellow color from eggs and turmeric. Try presenting it spooned over sliced, roasted Yukon Gold potatoes. The dish's intensity is addictive, and its velvety richness pairs naturally with ceviche's clean flavors and acidity. yield: 6 servings

HUANCAINA SAUCE

3 tablespoons vegetable oil

1 white onion, coarsely chopped

3 cloves garlic, chopped

2 hard-boiled eggs, sliced

1 tablespoon ground turmeric

1 can (12 ounces) evaporated milk

3 ounces feta cheese

3 ounces cream cheese

10 saltine crackers, crumbled

Salt

2 pounds Roasted Papas Amarilla (page 88)

To make the sauce, heat the oil in a sauté pan or skillet, add the onion, garlic, and eggs, and sauté over medium-low heat until the onions are translucent, about 5 minutes. Stir in the turmeric and sauté for another 2 minutes. Stir in the evaporated milk and simmer for 3 minutes. Remove the pan from the heat and let the mixture cool briefly. Transfer the mixture to a blender. Add the feta, cream cheese, and crackers, and blend on low speed until smooth. Season with salt to taste. Cover and chill in the refrigerator overnight. Bring to room temperature or heat and serve over the Roasted Papas Amarilla.

solterito

This classic ceviche accompaniment is a colorful salad worthy of its own spotlight. There are many variations of the dish, but they all usually contain lima beans, cheese, tomato, potato, and sometimes fresh seaweed. The earthy flavors of the vegetables and richness of the salty queso blanco *cheese balance the acidity of any marinated fish.*

A soltero *is a person who is unmarried. Perhaps this vibrant crunchy salad, while perfectly delicious on its own, is searching for its perfect mate—a tart, vibrant, bright ceviche.* yield: 6 to 8 servings

⅓ pound baby Yukon Gold potatoes, rinsed and scrubbed

Extra virgin olive oil for roasting

Salt

SOLTERITO

1 pint (about 7 ounces) grape tomatoes, thinly sliced

6 ounces frozen lima beans, thawed

4 ounces *queso blanco* cheese, finely diced

¼ cup raw butternut squash, finely julienned

¼ cup pitted Alfonso olives (see page 121), julienned

¼ cup fresh snow peas, trimmed and julienned

3 tablespoons chopped fresh flat-leaf parsley leaves

1 tablespoon finely chopped fresh chives

1 ounce fresh Fresno chiles (about 3 whole), finely diced

VINAIGRETTE

2 tablespoons red wine vinegar

½ teaspoon panca pepper paste (see page 122)

¼ cup extra virgin olive oil

½ teaspoon sugar

½ teaspoon salt, plus more as needed

Freshly ground black pepper

Preheat the oven to 350°F. Toss the potatoes with oil on a baking sheet and sprinkle with salt. Roast until fork-tender, about 20 minutes. Remove from the oven, let cool, and dice.

In a large bowl, gently toss together the solterito ingredients and the roasted potatoes until just combined.

To make the vinaigrette, whisk together the vinegar and panca paste in a small bowl until smooth. While whisking, drizzle in the olive oil. Add the sugar, salt, and pepper to taste and whisk until smooth. Pour over the salad and gently toss to coat; taste for seasoning and add salt if needed. Serve as an accompaniment to ceviche.

peruvian tuna causa

Every time I've eaten causa, a layered, chilled potato salad, it's been completely different. The very first time I tried it, at a Peruvian restaurant in Miami, it was made with layers of mashed white potatoes, chopped olives, and tomatoes. The next time, prepared at the home of a Peruvian friend, it came molded in a cup, with crabmeat, a layer of mashed yellow potato that had been cooked with saffron, and a layer of mashed white potato. When I encountered it on my travels in Peru, it was made with blue potatoes and tuna salad. Apparently, the recipe changes from town to town. This dish borrows a little from each version I have tasted.

Causa should be made at least one day in advance to allow the flavors to permeate the potatoes. It can be made in individual cups, but my preference is to make it in a loaf pan, which allows you to cut attractive slices, like a terrine. Imported canned tuna from Spain is best. yield: 8 servings

2 pounds Yukon Gold potatoes, scrubbed clean

1 pound baking potatoes, scrubbed clean

¾ cup mayonnaise

Juice of 1 lemon

Salt

TUNA MIXTURE

1 can (1 pound) high-quality imported tuna packed in olive oil, drained

1 can (approximately 2 ounces) anchovies in oil, drained

½ cup virgin olive oil

2 tablespoons red wine vinegar

2 cloves garlic

2 tablespoons minced drained capers

2 tablespoon minced fresh flat-leaf parsley

1 red bell pepper, roasted, peeled, seeded, and diced (see page 108)

⅓ cup black Alfonso (see page 121), niçoise, or kalamata olives, pitted and diced small

Preheat the oven to 350°F. Wrap each whole potato in aluminum foil and bake for 1 hour or until fork-tender. Remove the potatoes from the oven and let cool slightly before unwrapping and peeling. Put the potatoes through a ricer (or mash with a potato masher or fork), keeping the yellow and white varieties in separate bowls. Fold 6 tablespoons of the mayonnaise and half the lemon juice into the potatoes in each bowl. Season to taste with salt. Set aside.

In a bowl, combine all of the tuna mixture ingredients. Stir until well combined and set aside.

Grease a 9 by 4-inch loaf pan with a little olive oil and line it with plastic wrap. (The wrap should extend over the edges of the pan by a couple of inches on all sides.) Layer half of the mashed Yukon Gold potatoes in the bottom of the pan and spread evenly. Spread half of the tuna mixture on top of the potato layer and then add all of the mashed baking potatoes in one layer over the tuna. Add a final layer of the remaining tuna mixture, and finish with a layer of the remaining Yukon Gold potatoes. Fold the plastic wrap over to cover the top layer, and chill in the refrigerator for at least 2 hours or overnight. To serve, unfold the top covering of plastic wrap and gently invert the loaf pan onto a serving platter. Carefully remove the plastic wrap, and cut the *causa* into slices.

roasted camote or papas amarilla

Plain Roasted Camote (the Spanish word for "sweet potatoes") or Papas Amarilla sprinkled with salt are perfect on their own as a simple accompaniment to most of my ceviches, especially the more intricate recipes such as the Indian Mussels with Pineapple Juice and Curry (page 74) or Peruvian Orange Duck (page 81). For a richer, more intense side dish, try Papas Amarilla with Huancaina Sauce (page 83) or Ocopa Sauce (opposite) ladled over. yield: 2 pounds (6 servings)

2 pounds yams or sweet
potatoes or Yukon Gold
potatoes, each about the
same size, scrubbed clean

Salt for sprinkling

Preheat the oven to 350°F. Wrap each whole potato in aluminum foil and bake for 1 hour, or until fork-tender. Remove the potatoes from the oven and let cool slightly before unwrapping and peeling. Cut into 1-inch-thick slices, sprinkle with salt, and serve at room temperature with any ceviche.

papas ocopa

A Peruvian accompaniment to ceviche, Papas Ocopa is Roasted Papas Amarilla ladled with a thick sauce of evaporated milk, walnuts, and feta cheese. The richness of the Ocopa Sauce is a perfect balance to the sharp acidity of just about any ceviche. I've included both panca pepper and aji amarillo paste to add some heat, while the dried shrimp will mimic the seafood tones of the accompanying ceviche. yield: 6 servings

OCOPA SAUCE

1 white onion, diced

1 red bell pepper, seeded and diced

4 cloves garlic, chopped

1/2 cup virgin olive oil

4 ounces dried shrimp (see page 121)

3 tablespoons panca pepper paste (see page 122)

2 tablespoons aji amarillo paste (see page 121)

1 tablespoon ground turmeric

2 cans (12 ounces each) evaporated milk

1 cup walnut halves

8 ounces feta cheese

6 sprigs huacatay (see page 121) or mint, coarsely chopped

2 pounds Roasted Papas Amarilla (opposite)

Alfonso (see page 121), niçoise, or kalamata olives for garnish

To make the sauce, in a deep sauté pan over medium heat, sauté the onion, bell pepper, and garlic in the olive oil for about 5 minutes, or until soft. Add the shrimp, panca pepper paste, aji paste, and the turmeric and cook for an additional 3 minutes, until the pastes are well incorporated. Add the evaporated milk, bring to a simmer, and cover. Let the mixture simmer for about 40 minutes. Remove the pan from the heat and let cool for 1 hour. Combine the milk mixture in a blender with the walnuts, feta, and huacatay and purée until smooth. Pour the sauce at room temperature or slightly heated over the Roasted Papas Amarilla and garnish with the olives.

yuca frita

Also called cassava or manioc, yuca is a tubular root vegetable with white flesh and a rough, brown skin; it can be found at most specialty markets. Frying it creates a dry, fluffy interior, similar to that of a potato, but with a sweeter, more buttery flavor, and a crisp exterior that contrasts perfectly with the silky texture of ceviche. I admit that these fried yuca matchsticks do take a little elbow grease, but don't give up. If you serve them fresh and hot, they are well worth the extra effort. yield: 6 servings

2 pounds fresh yuca, peeled and soaked in cold water (see page 123)

8 cups vegetable oil

Salt for sprinkling

On a mandoline, slice the yuca into matchsticks. If you don't have a mandoline, cut the yuca crosswise into slices then stack the slices and cut crosswise again into matchsticks. In a stockpot, heat the oil to 350°F. When hot, cook the yuca in small batches until golden brown. Drain on paper towels and sprinkle with salt. Serve immediately.

quinoa amontillado

Often referred to as "the mother grain," quinoa has been an important ingredient in South American cooking since the time of the Incas, but not until recently did it become popular in American cuisine. I think you'll really enjoy trying quinoa as an accompaniment to ceviche, not only for its taste and bite, but also for its health benefits: it has the highest protein content of any grain. yield: 6 servings

1 pound quinoa (see page 122)

3 cloves garlic, minced

¼ cup virgin olive oil

1 small red bell pepper, seeded and diced small

½ cup finely chopped fresh flat-leaf parsley

½ cup black Alfonso (see page 121), niçoise, or kalamata olives, pitted and diced small

Pinch of salt

Rinse the quinoa in a bowl of cold water by rubbing it between your fingers. Drain and repeat until the water is clear. Place the quinoa and enough water to cover in a medium saucepan and bring to a boil over high heat. Lower the heat and simmer for 10 minutes, or until the quinoa is translucent. Drain and rinse under cold water. Drain again and set aside.

In a small sauté pan over high heat, sauté the garlic in the oil for 1 minute. Add the bell pepper and continue to sauté for about 2 minutes, until soft. Blend the sautéed mixture and the remaining ingredients into the quinoa and serve at room temperature.

chulpe

This crunchy, addictive side dish is typical of Ecuadorian ceviche restaurants with the addition of pork rind. Although American palates might bristle at the amount of deep-frying involved, as they say, once you've had it, you just can't stop. I had to think twice about including this recipe in the book, but judging by the response from my kitchen staff (they refer to it as "corn crack"), I knew I couldn't leave it out. You may walk into my restaurant one day and find it on the menu or served at the bar.

South America grows more than twenty varieties of corn. Chulpe, the medium-sized yellow variety, can be found in Latin grocery stores. Be sure to dry the corn very well after soaking, as any water on the corn will splatter when you drop it into the hot oil. yield: 2 quarts

1 pound dried chulpe corn kernels

10 ounces sliced applewood smoked bacon

Vegetable oil for frying

1 1/2 large red onions, peeled and thinly sliced on a mandoline

Put the corn kernels in a large bowl and cover with warm water. Soak, stirring occasionally, for 1 hour. Drain well in a colander and pat dry with paper towels.

Preheat the oven to 350°F. Put the bacon slices on a baking sheet and roast in the oven until crisp, 20 to 25 minutes. Transfer to a paper towel–lined plate to drain, and then chop them into 1-inch pieces. Leave the oven on at 350°F.

Fill a deep heavy-bottomed saucepan with 4 inches of vegetable oil, attach a frying thermometer to the pan, and heat the oil to 375°F. Working in batches, quickly fry the corn, just until it begins to pop and is coated with oil, about 15 seconds. Be careful—it will splatter. Transfer the fried corn to a baking sheet and roast it in the oven until light golden brown and crunchy, about 30 minutes.

Working in batches, deep-fry the onion slices in the same oil until very dark brown, nearly burnt, about 2 minutes. Transfer to a paper towel–lined plate to drain.

In a large bowl, gently toss together the toasted corn, bacon pieces, and fried onions until combined. Serve at room temperature as an accompaniment to ceviche.

corn nuts

For most Americans, the name "corn nuts" brings to mind the small bags of salty, crunchy nuggets that you find hanging on checkout-line hooks at your local convenience store. Have you ever wondered who thought of this brilliant snack? Peruvians claim the original interpretation—dried corn kernels that are reconstituted, boiled, then fried and tossed with salt—another perfect flavor-texture complement to ceviche.

There are many varieties of corn that work for this recipe. I like to use chulpe, a medium-sized dried corn native to Peru. However, since this corn might be difficult to find outside of Latin grocery stores, you have my permission to resort to the ready-made corn nuts. Just be sure to pick up the plain salted variety and avoid the overly processed flavors. yield: 2 to 3 cups

1 cup dried chulpe corn kernels

Vegetable oil for coating

Salt for sprinkling

Soak the corn kernels in hot water for two hours. Preheat the oven to 350°F. Drain the kernels in a colander and pat dry with paper towels. Place the kernels on a baking sheet and cover them with vegetable oil, stirring them around with your fingers to coat them evenly. Toast the kernels in the oven for approximately 30 minutes, stirring occasionally, until they are golden and crisp. Sprinkle with salt to taste.

popcorn

This recipe will remind you that popcorn didn't always come in tightly sealed microwavable bags that pop in eight minutes flat. As with most kitchen tasks, it's good to remember and experience cooking things the old-fashioned way. So don't be scared off by using a hot pan and a little bit of oil to pop your corn. The result is fresher, tastier, and much more fun. As you know by now, popcorn is the perfect accompaniment to ceviche. Its contrasting salty-dry crunch and chew works to cleanse the palate between bites of silky, citrusy ceviche. I like to add garlic salt for an extra punch. yield: about 5 quarts

2 tablespoons vegetable oil	²/₃ cup unpopped corn kernels	Garlic salt

Cover the bottom of a 6-quart stockpot with the oil, add the corn kernels, and cover. Let the pan sit on high to medium-high heat until the kernels start popping. Shake the pan regularly, returning it to the stove until the popping slows. Turn off the heat and let the remaining kernels pop before removing the lid. Season with garlic salt to taste.

basics

cleaning conch

Those golden, intricately spiraled shells that we've all held up to our ears while reminiscing of vacations by the sea don't just hold soothing sounds of the ocean. They're actually home to the culinary treasure, conch. Cleaning and tenderizing conch can be a bit of work, but once you've tasted it, the work will become a labor of love. Conch is actually touted as an aphrodisiac. To this day, conch remains the single most delicious seafood I've ever eaten and its incredibly sweet freshness is perfect for ceviche.

It is extremely difficult to get fresh conch. In 1983, Queen Conch was named an endangered species and, because of this, many other related conch species were also placed under governmental import/export restriction. Since then, the season, which typically runs from November through June in high-export countries like Jamaica, has often been "closed," causing the frozen variety to be an easier find in the United States.

Luckily, there are some admirable individuals who have made a life's work out of protecting this sea delicacy. One of these individuals is my friend Steve Garca, who works for White Water International and brings the treasures of the Caicos Conch Farm into the United States. Located on the Island of Providenciales, in the Turks and Caicos Islands, the farm breeds about one million conch each year, selling to chefs and retailers, as well as working to repopulate the Queen Conch in the Caribbean.

When purchasing frozen conch, look for the label "Grade A" and make sure to peek into the typical 5-pound box to check for freezer burn before making a purchase. To clean frozen conch, defrost it and rinse it under cold water until its slimy texture is washed away. Place it on a cutting board and trim away any black patches of skin or flap-like growths, ending up with only the grayish and white meat of the muscle. Do not refreeze conch after thawing; its flavor will suffer dramatically. Place the trimmed conch between two pieces of wax paper and pound it with the smooth end of a meat mallet until it has almost doubled in size, is smooth, and is about ¼ inch thick. Prepare per recipe instructions.

sautéing scallops

There are many different species of scallops, large sea scallops and small bay scallops being the two most common categories. Although you can purchase large sea scallops and chop them for use in ceviches, bay scallops are actually slightly sweeter and I sometimes prefer their uniform shape and smooth, marshmallow-like texture.

The following method will produce a nice, slightly seared exterior and a tender interior. The searing creates a protective barrier, halting the action of the citrus juices in ceviche marinades and helping to maintain the scallops' light texture.

Scallops do not require a lot of cooking time. Simply sauté them quickly in a skillet, over medium heat with a little bit of oil, until they've released their juices and become barely opaque, about 2 minutes. Do not cook more than can fit in a single layer in your pan at any one time. You may need to work in batches. When cooked, lay the scallops out in a single layer on a baking sheet to stop the cooking and allow them to cool. Scallops can be cooked 1 day in advance, covered, and stored in the refrigerator.

blanching scallops

This cooking procedure is a way to manipulate the amount of acid the scallops will absorb from a ceviche marinade. Blanching actually seals and protects the scallops' inside texture while still allowing some flavor from the marinade to be absorbed. If you store the scallops along with the clam juice in the refrigerator, they will remain moist.

Amount of scallops per recipe instructions

½ cup clam juice per pound of scallops

In a deep skillet over high heat, blanch half the scallops in half the clam juice for about 3 minutes, stirring often, until opaque. Reserve cooked scallops in a bowl and repeat the cooking process with the remaining scallops and clam juice. If not using immediately, refrigerate the scallops with the clam juice for up to 1 day.

shucking oysters

Shucking oysters does take some practice, but life will be better once you've mastered this skill. If you can, purchase shucking gloves rather than using a loose kitchen towel. You will be able to grip the oyster better without fearing a harmful slip of the knife.

Brush the oysters clean, being careful of their sharp shells and rinsing with ice-cold water if necessary. While shucking each oyster, keep the other oysters on ice. Working over a bowl to catch any juices, grasp one oyster by its hinge with a kitchen towel or with shucking gloves. Insert an oyster knife into the seam, where the top and bottom shells meet, and gently rock and twist the knife until the hinge breaks open. You do not want to disturb the flesh of the oyster. Once the hinge breaks open, slide the knife along the underside of the top shell until you reach the muscle that holds the top and bottom shells together. Cut through this muscle and rinse the oyster to remove any pieces of shell. Now, detach the oyster from the bottom part of the shell. Repeat with remaining oysters and prepare them per recipe instructions.

roasting clams or oysters

Roasting is the easiest way to open clams and oysters. The quick, high heat lures them out of their shells without overcooking. Roasting clams and oysters is particularly effective in making ceviche because the flavor remains concentrated in the meat of the shellfish rather than being lost to a pot of boiling water.

Amount of clams or oysters
per recipe instructions

Preheat the oven to 450°F. Place the clams or oysters on a baking sheet and bake on the middle rack of the oven for about 6 minutes, until most of the shells have opened. Remove them from the oven. Tap the unopened shells with a pair of kitchen tongs; this will help them to open. When the clams or oysters have cooled, over a bowl to catch any juices, use a clam or oyster knife to remove the flesh from the shells.

cooking octopus

There is a Spanish technique of placing a cork into the poaching liquid when cooking octopus to increase its tenderness. Be it fact or fiction, I always practice this method and believe it to be true. If you have the time, it's worth it to seek out fresh octopus rather than previously frozen. Also, based on my experience, Portuguese octopus has the best flavor and quality. Although I like to spice up other seafood poaching liquids with Latin flavorings, water works just fine here since the octopus's thick skin will not absorb any flavor during cooking. That said, the octopus itself imparts a rich, gelatinous character to the water, making it a great prize for poaching other seafood, cooking rice, or flavoring soups, stews, or stocks.

Because the look and texture of the octopus's tentacles are important to the dish, to ensure that the tentacles' skin remains intact, follow these rules: Use a pot just large enough to hold the octopus to minimize movement during cooking; cook at a gentle simmer, never at a rapid boil; and carefully follow the procedures in the recipe for cooling the octopus in the water and removing it by its head.

Amount of octopus per recipe instructions, preferably fresh

1 wine cork

If you've purchased frozen octopus, thaw it first before cleaning. To clean the octopus, rinse it under cold water. Squeeze your fingers lengthwise along the tentacles, from the body down to the tips, until their slimy texture is washed away. Place the octopus in a stockpot just large enough to hold it, cover completely with cold water, add the wine cork, and bring to a simmer over medium heat. Do not let the water boil, or the skin of the tentacles will peel off during cooking. Let the mixture simmer, covered, for about 1½ hours; the tentacles will become softer during cooking and will feel tender to the touch when done. Remove the pot from the heat and let it cool. If you need to speed along the cooling process, add some ice cubes to the liquid. When the octopus is cool, remove it gently from the liquid by grabbing its head with your hands. Octopus can be cooked 1 day in advance and stored in a covered container and refrigerated until ready to use. Let the poaching liquid cool and store it for future use. It will keep for a couple of days in the refrigerator. Alternatively, it can be frozen in small batches for longer storage.

blanching shrimp

To the average observer, the spices and seasonings added to this highly flavored poaching liquid might seem excessive. I assure you, you will enjoy the results! In the French tradition, fish or seafood might be poached in a court bouillon enhanced with white wine, bay leaf, and peppercorns. This recipe's Latin spin on poaching liquid really infuses the shrimp with vibrant flavor and brings out their fresh briny overtones. My trick of splitting the shrimp in half lengthwise along the vein causes them to curl up during poaching, resulting in beautifully unusual spirals—perfect for holding ceviche marinades and sauces in every bite.

POACHING LIQUID

5 quarts water

1 lemon, thinly sliced

2 tablespoons Worcestershire sauce

¼ cup Tabasco sauce

¾ cup pickling spice

3 tablespoons salt

2 tablespoons whole black peppercorns

Amount of shrimp per recipe instructions

In a 6-quart stockpot, combine all of the poaching liquid ingredients and bring to a boil over high heat. Decrease the heat and simmer, covered, for 20 to 30 minutes so that the flavors can steep.

If you have purchased frozen shrimp, you will want to defrost them before peeling and deveining by rinsing them under cold running water. While the liquid is steeping, peel the shrimp by grasping the legs, pulling to one side, and removing the entire shell. Pull off the shrimp tails. Run a knife along the center of the outer curve of the shrimp from the head to the tail end, all the way through, slicing the shrimp in half lengthwise along the vein. Pull out or wash away the dark vein. This may be easier in ice water or under cold running water. (Some stores now sell shell-on shrimp with a cut already made down the back of the shell and the veins removed, which makes this process easier.)

When the poaching liquid has finished steeping, let it cool slightly, and strain it through a fine-mesh strainer into a clean pot. Bring the liquid back to a boil over high heat. Working in small batches (about 4 ounces each), place the split shrimp into a pasta basket or mesh strainer and dunk them into the boiling liquid for about 1 minute, or until they begin to curl. They will begin to turn white and opaque, but will not be fully cooked. Remove the shrimp from the liquid and place them, spread out, on a baking sheet to cool. Do not shock them in an ice bath or in cold water as this will wash off the flavors of the poaching liquid. Bring the liquid back up to a boil again before adding another batch of shrimp. When finished, discard the poaching liquid. Shrimp can be blanched 1 day in advance and stored in a covered container in the refrigerator.

mussel stock

Mussels are very inexpensive, yet they still impart a wonderfully strong sea flavor to stock, and the resulting liquid is a perfect addition to ceviche. While the mussels are steeping, gently shake the covered stockpot to help open the shells. This will release the maximum amount of briny flavor into the water. yield: about 5 1/2 quarts

5 quarts water

1 (750-ml) bottle dry white wine

2 carrots, peeled and diced large

1 onion, peeled and diced large

3 celery ribs, washed and diced large

1 tablespoon whole black peppercorns

2 pounds mussels

In a 6-quart stockpot, combine all of the ingredients, except the mussels, and bring to a boil over high heat.

While waiting for the liquid to boil, clean and debeard the mussels by rinsing them under cold running water and scrubbing them to remove any dirt or grit. Pull off and discard the beard, the black fibers that grow from the shell of the mussel.

Add the mussels to the boiling liquid and stir to combine. Immediately cover, remove from the heat, and let steep for about 20 minutes. Remove the cover and drain the mussels in a colander set over a large bowl to reserve the stock. The mussel stock can be cooled and stored for up to 2 days in the refrigerator. Alternatively, it can be frozen in small batches for longer storage. Prepare the cooked mussels per recipe instructions.

lobster stock

Making a great lobster stock requires an investment of both time and money. But it is an investment that will reap a tableful of rewards, as in my Honduran Fire and Ice Lobster ceviche (page 65). Don't skimp on the amount of sherry, as the three cups will add a distinctive undertone to the stock, which you can also freeze for future use in sauces or soups. yield: about 3 quarts

5 pounds lobster shells, split

1 cup (8 ounces) unsalted butter

6 carrots, peeled and coarsely chopped

6 stalks celery, washed and coarsely chopped

4 white onions, peeled and coarsely chopped

3 cloves garlic, halved

3 cups dry sherry (see page 123)

1 tablespoon crushed red pepper flakes

4 bay leaves

1 bunch thyme, tied with kitchen twine

1 bunch parsley, tied with kitchen twine

¼ cup tomato paste

Thoroughly wash out the lobster shells. Melt the butter in a stockpot over medium-high heat. Add the lobster shells, carrots, celery, onions, and garlic and sauté, stirring continuously, until softened, about 20 minutes. Add the sherry and deglaze the pot. Cook for 5 minutes longer. Add the pepper flakes, bay leaves, thyme, parsley, tomato paste, and 1 gallon water and bring to a boil. Decrease the heat to low and simmer for 2 hours, periodically skimming off any fat and impurities that rise to the surface. Pour the liquid through a fine-mesh strainer. Discard the lobster shells, vegetables, and herbs and use the stock as directed in the recipe.

blanching lobster

The key to pleasantly chewy lobster meat with a smooth texture is to make sure the lobster is alive and kicking when you blanch it. If not, you'll end up with meat that is gummy and grainy. If you're a first-timer, don't be timid when plunging the lobster to its fate. Just think how happy it'll be when it gets bathed in a sauce of aji amarillo and citrus, as in my Paella Ceviche on page 62.

Amount of lobster per recipe instructions

2 tablespoons salt

In a 12-quart covered stockpot, bring 2 gallons of water to a boil (or enough to cover 1 to 2 lobsters without the pot being crowded). Add the salt, cover, and boil for about 5 minutes per pound. With tongs, remove the lobster from the water, discard the liquid, and place the lobster in a bowl in the refrigerator to fully cool, about 2 hours. Prepare per recipe instructions.

calamari ribbons

When you see calamari served in a restaurant, it's always in typical ringlet form, circular slices cut from its tubelike body. I wanted to create a different preparation, so after some experimenting, I came up with this easy method for creating ribbons of calamari rather than ringlets. It's very difficult to thinly slice calamari (a desirable form for ceviche) when it's raw, but freezing it in a block makes slicing on a mandoline a breeze. You can attempt cutting very thin slices with a sharp knife, but the effect will not be the same.

Amount of calamari per
recipe instructions

Thoroughly wash the calamari bodies inside and out, remove the tentacle ends, and cut them lengthwise along one side to make one sheetlike piece. Repeat this process until all tubes are split and flattened into sheets. Place the calamari sheets in a loaf pan layered on top of each other and freeze them overnight. When frozen, remove the calamari from the freezer and slice very thin, preferably on a mandoline. Fully defrost the calamari slices by running them under cold water. To cook them, bring 1 gallon of salted water to a boil.

Working in small batches, place the calamari slices in a strainer and dip into the boiling water for about 10 seconds, or until curled up and opaque. Let cool in the refrigerator spread out in a single layer on a baking sheet. Store the cooled calamari in a covered container in the refrigerator for up to 4 days.

fried plantains

The garlic flavoring gives these plantain chips an intriguing and unusual twist. The plaintains should be sliced with a mandoline. yield: 4 servings

3 cups canola oil

2 green plantains (see page 122), peeled and very thinly sliced lengthwise

Salt for sprinkling

Garlic powder for sprinkling

Heat the oil to 350°F in a deep-fat fryer or a large, heavy-bottomed saucepan. When the oil is hot, add the plantain slices one at a time; do not overcrowd the pan or the oil will not stay hot enough. (Cook in batches if necessary.) Deep-fry until golden, 3 to 4 minutes.

Remove the chips with a wire-mesh strainer and drain on paper towels. Sprinkle with the salt and garlic powder and let cool.

roasting jalapeño chiles, bell peppers, tomatoes, or onions

Roasting changes the taste profile of any ingredient and chiles and bell peppers are no exception. After roasting, do not use water to rinse off the charred skins, as this will wash away the deep, smoky flavor; your fingers will do nicely.

Amount of chiles, bell peppers, tomatoes, or onions specified in recipe

Place the whole chiles, bell peppers, tomatoes, or onions on a grill rack over a barbecue's open flame; hold with tongs over a gas burner; or set on a baking sheet under a broiler. Roast, turning occasionally, until the skins are blistered and blackened all over, but before the flesh underneath the skin becomes charred. Transfer to a bowl and cover tightly with plastic wrap. Let steam for 10 to 15 minutes.

When cool enough to handle, remove the skins with your fingers or the tip of a knife. (If you have sensitive skin, wear rubber gloves when handling chiles.) For the jalapeños, peppers, or tomatoes, remove and discard the stems, seeds (unless the recipe instructs otherwise), and internal ribs, and use as directed. Warning: Do not touch your face or eyes after handling chiles, until you have thoroughly washed your hands.

pickled carrots

These tasty carrots have a very long shelf life in the refrigerator, and will add a welcome crunch to salads and sandwiches. yield: about 4 cups

2 cups white distilled vinegar

3 tablespoons honey

2 tablespoons salt

7 ounces matchstick julienned carrots (3 to 4 regular size or 2 extra-large)

Zest of 1 lemon

Put the vinegar, honey, and salt in a saucepan and bring to a boil over medium-high heat. Put the carrot julienne and lemon zest in a large nonreactive bowl. Pour the hot liquid over the carrots, toss gently, and let stand for 5 minutes. Add 3 cups crushed ice to the mixture and toss. Once completely cooled, transfer the carrots and liquid to an airtight container and store in the refrigerator until ready to use.

pickled jalapeños

I use a lot of these, both mixed into dishes and as a tangy garnish. I like to pickle my own, rather than buying them, because I prefer including the ripe, red jalapeños in addition to the green ones. Don't be scared off by the heat you might expect from this accompaniment. The pickling actually takes away most of the high-level spiciness in the peppers, leaving a mellow warmth with just enough kick.

Stored in a glass container with a tight-fitting lid, these jalapeños will keep for about a month in the refrigerator. Any longer, and the peppers will lose their characteristic crunch and freshness.

yield: about 2½ cups

3 cups white vinegar

¼ cup sugar

¼ cup salt

8 ounces red jalapeños (approximately 12)

8 ounces green jalapeños (approximately 12)

8 ounces shallots (approximately 6), chopped fine

In a nonreactive bowl, whisk together the vinegar, sugar, and salt and set aside. Thinly slice the jalapeños crosswise into rounds with a Japanese mandoline or a sharp knife. The seeds should be left in. Pour the marinade over the jalapeños and shallots in a glass container. Gently mix, cover with a tight-fitting lid, and refrigerate for at least 24 hours before using.

candied orange rind

No chef would recommend eating a bitter handful of raw orange rind. But that recommendation would likely change if candied rind came into question. Many home cooks shy away from candying their own citrus rind because, at first glance, the process seems daunting. Don't worry; although candying may take some time, the process is actually quite simple. Repeated boiling transforms the bitter rind into an unexpected sweet that's perfectly enjoyable on its own. Be careful to save enough to top some of my stronger-flavored ceviches, like kingfish or pompano, where candied orange rind adds a welcome sugary crunch. yield: about 1 cup

4 large oranges, quartered, flesh removed, and rinds cut into thin, long strips

5 cups sugar

In a stockpot, bring 2 quarts of water to a boil over high heat. Add the orange rind, cook for 3 minutes until it begins to get limp, and drain. Repeat this process two more times, using clean water each time. After boiling three times, bring 4 cups of the sugar and 4 cups of water to a boil, stirring well to dissolve the sugar. Add the rind, decrease the heat to a simmer, and cook for about 30 minutes. Drain the rind and place on a flat surface lined with paper towels. In a bowl, toss the rind with the remaining 1 cup of sugar until coated. Spread on a parchment paper–lined baking sheet and let dry.

Note: For candied kumquats, instead of the orange, substitute 8 ounces of whole kumquats sliced into thin rounds (seeds removed). They can be tossed in sugar after cooking in syrup and dried like the orange rind, or they can be cooled and stored directly in the syrup, as for the Tuna Watermelon Ceviche (page 77).

crispy ginger

This creates a nice sudden heat flash on the palate. Add it to ceviches or salads—this crispy ginger pairs nicely with lean foods. yield: 2 tablespoons

2 tablespoons peeled fresh
ginger, finely chopped

Vegetable oil for frying

Fill a small, heavy-bottomed saucepan with 1 inch of vegetable oil and heat over medium-high heat until hot but not smoking. Drop a piece of ginger in the oil to test it; it should bubble gently. Add the ginger and fry, stirring, until deep golden brown, about 4 minutes. Use a fine-mesh strainer to remove the ginger and transfer it to a paper towel–lined plate to drain. Store the ginger in an airtight container lined with a paper towel to keep crisp. It will keep for several days.

crunchy garlic and garlic oil

One day I was trying to make a quick garlic-flavored oil, and as it turns out, this crunchy garlic is now a garnish used often in all of my kitchens. The garlic oil is one of those basics I couldn't live without because it's so easy and adds so much flavor to a variety of dishes. yield: ¼ cup crunchy garlic, 2 cups garlic oil

20 cloves garlic, peeled and
ends trimmed

2 cups vegetable oil

1 teaspoon salt

Put the garlic, oil and salt in the jar of a blender and pulse for 30 seconds to break up the garlic. Turn the blender on high and purée until the mixture is very smooth and emulsified and there are no visible pieces of garlic left, about 5 minutes. Transfer to a heavy-bottomed nonstick pan over medium-high heat. Stir the oil with a wooden spoon as it heats and begins to separate. Continue stirring constantly as the garlic begins to clump together and do not walk away; garlic can stick to the pan and burn if not stirred constantly while it browns. Cook until the garlic turns a light golden brown but no further; it becomes bitter if it gets too dark. Strain the garlic through a fine-mesh strainer and turn it out onto a paper towel–lined plate to cool. Store the crunchy garlic in an airtight container lined with a paper towel and the garlic-flavored oil in an airtight container at room temperature. It will keep for several days.

dried mushroom–adobo rub

You'd think the earthy flavor of mushrooms would dominate in this rub, but it doesn't. Instead, the mushroom flavor transforms the spices into a sweet, rich mix that is hard to classify but is easy to enjoy. I like using it for my Beef Tenderloin with Citrus-Truffle Mayonniase ceviche (page 78) or simply to coat white-meat chicken, chayote, or scallops. yield: 1¹/₈ cups

2 to 3 ounces dried porcini mushrooms

¼ cup sugar

3 tablespoons kosher salt

2 tablespoons ground coriander

2 tablespoons paprika

1 tablespoon coarsely ground black pepper

1 tablespoon ground chipotle pepper

1 tablespoon mustard powder

1 teaspoon ground nutmeg

1 teaspoon ground aniseeds

Grind the dried porcinis to a powder in a food processor. In a bowl, thoroughly mix the porcinis with the rest of the ingredients. Use at once or transfer to an airtight jar and store for up to 6 months.

lemon oil

I've used this versatile oil for years. It's good for dressing greens, marinating fish, and incorporating into mojos. I am sure that once you have tried it, you will find as many uses for it around the kitchen as I have. yield: 2 cups

2 cups vegetable oil   ¼ cup lemon zest   2 teaspoons ground turmeric

Combine the oil, lemon zest, and turmeric in a saucepan and gently warm over low heat for 1 hour to infuse the oil with the lemon flavor. Let the oil cool to room temperature. Use at once or store in a covered container in the refrigerator for up to 2 weeks.

RECOMMENDED SOURCES OF SEAFOOD AND SPECIALTY ITEMS

ATLANTA

Harry's Farmers Market

alpharetta:
1180 Upper Hembree Road
Roswell, GA 30076
(770) 664-6300

gwinnett:
2025 Satellite Point
Duluth, GA 30136
(770) 416-6900

cobb:
70 Powers Ferry Road
Marietta, GA 30067
(770) 578-4400

Star Provisions
www.starprovisions.com
1198 Howell Mill Road NW
Atlanta, GA 30318
(404) 365-0410

Whole Foods Market
www.wholefoodsmarket.com
2111 Briarcliff Road NE
Atlanta, GA 30329
(404) 634-7800

5930 Roswell Road
Atlanta, GA 30328
(404) 236-0810

BOSTON

Cape Cod Shellfish and
Seafood Company
33-35 Boston Fish Pier
Boston, MA 02210
(617) 423-1555
*Oysters, clams, and various
seafood.*

James Hook & Company
www.jameshooklobster.com
15 Northern Avenue
Boston, MA 02210
(617) 423-5501

Marblehead Lobster
Company
www.marblehead-lobster.
com
Beacon and Orne Street
Marblehead, MA 01945
(888) 842-7570
Mail-order lobsters.

Steve Connolly Seafood
Company
www.steveconnolly
seafood.com
34 Newmarket Square
Boston, MA 02118
(617) 427-7700
*Wide range of New England fish
and shellfish.*

CHICAGO

Burhop's Seafood
www.burhops.com
1515 Sheridan Road
Wilmette, IL 60091
(847) 256-6400

Father & Son Plaza
609 West North Avenue
Chicago, IL 60610
(312) 642-8600

Fox & Obel Food Market
www.fox-obel.com
401 E. Illinois Street
Chicago, IL 60611
(312) 410-7301

L. Isaacson & Stein Fish
Company
www.isaacsonandstein.com
800 West Fulton Street
Chicago, IL 60607
(312) 421-2444

Treasure Island Foods
www.tifoods.com
3460 North Broadway
Chicago, IL 60657
(773) 327-3880

1639 North Wells Street
Chicago, IL 60614
(312) 642-1105

2121 N Clybourn
Chicago, IL 60614
(773) 880-8880

75 West Elm Street
Chicago, IL 60610
(312) 440-1144

680 North Lake Shore Drive
Chicago, IL 60611
(312) 664-0400

Whole Foods Market
www.wholefoodsmarket.com

gold coast:
30 West Huron Street
Chicago, IL 60654
(312) 932-9600

lakeview:
3300 North Ashland Avenue
Chicago, IL 60657
(773) 244-4200

lincoln park:
1550 N. Kingsbury Street
Chicago, IL 60642
(312) 587-0648
*Suburban locations in Deerfield,
Evanston, Palatine, River Forest,
and Wheaton.*

DALLAS

Central Market
5750 E. Lovers Lane
Dallas, TX 75206
(214) 234-7000
*A variety of other locations in
the Dallas area.*

Simon David
Supermarket
7117 Inwood Road
Dallas, TX 75209
(214) 352-1781
*A variety of other locations
in the Dallas area.*

Whole Foods Market
www.wholefoodsmarket.com
2118 Abrams Road
Dallas, TX 75214
(214) 824-1744

11700 Preston Road
Dallas, TX 75230
(214) 361-8887

LOS ANGELES

Fish King
www.fishkingseafood.com
722 N. Glendale Avenue
Glendale, CA 91206
(818) 244-2161

Santa Monica Seafood
www.smseafood.com
1000 Wilshire Boulevard
Santa Monica, CA 90401
(310) 393-5244

99 Ranch Market
651 N. Euclid Street
Anaheim, CA 92801
(714) 776-8899
*A variety of other locations in
surrounding areas.*

Whole Foods Market
www.wholefoodsmarket.com

west los angeles:
11666 National Boulevard
Los Angeles, CA 90064
(310) 996-8840
*A variety of other locations in
Southern California.*

MIAMI

Captain Jim's Seafood
12950 West Dixie Highway
North Miami, FL 33161
(305) 892-2812

Norman Brothers Seafood
& Produce
www.normanbrothers.com
7621 Southwest 87th Avenue
Miami, FL 33173
(305) 274-9363

Waterfront Market
201 William Street
Key West, FL 33040
(305) 296-0778

Whole Foods Market
www.wholefoodsmarket.com
2000 North Federal Highway
Fort Lauderdale, FL 33305
(954) 565-5655

MINNEAPOLIS

Byerly's
www.lundsandbyerlys.com

original store:
5725 Duluth Street
Golden Valley, MN 55422
(763) 544-8846
*A variety of other locations in
the Twin Cities and surrounding
areas.*

Coastal Seafoods
74 S. Snelling Avenue
Saint Paul, MN 55105
(651) 698-4888

2330 S. Minnehaha Avenue
Minneapolis, MN 55404
(612) 724-7425

Lunds
3455 Vicksburg Lane
Plymouth, MN 55447
(763) 268-1624
A variety of other locations in the Twin Cities and surrounding areas.

NEW YORK

Dayboat Fisheries & Seafood Company
33 Fulton Street
New York, NY 10038
(212) 608-4590

The Gramercy Fish Company
383 2nd Avenue
New York, NY 10010
(212) 213-5557

The Lobster Place
www.lobsterplace.com
436 West 16th Street
New York, NY 10011
(212) 255-5672

Rosedale Fish & Oyster Market
1129 Lexington Avenue
New York, NY 10021
(212) 861-4323

M. Slavin & Sons Ltd
106 South Street
New York, NY 10038
(212) 233-4522

Spice House International Specialties
www.spicehouseint.com
46 Bethpage Road
Hicksville, NY 11801
(516) 942-7248

Whole Foods Market
www.wholefoodsmarket.com
250 7th Avenue at 24th Street
New York, NY 10001
(212) 924-5969

Wild Edibles
The Market at Grand Central Terminal
89 East 42nd Street
New York, NY 10017
(212) 687-4255

SAN FRANCISCO

Andronico's Market
www.andronicos.com
1200 Irving Street
San Francisco, CA 94122
(415) 661-3220

Hog Island Oyster Company
www.hogislandoysters.com
(415) 663-9218
Oysters and clams shipped within the continental United States.

Nikko Fish Company
2181 Irving Street
San Francisco, CA 94122
(415) 759-7254

Whole Foods Market
www.wholefoodsmarket.com
1765 California Street
San Francisco, CA 94109
(415) 674-0500
A variety of other locations in Northern California.

SEATTLE

Mutual Fish Company
www.mutualfish.com
2335 Rainier Avenue South
Seattle, WA 98144
(206) 322-4368

Uwajimaya Store
www.uwajimaya.com
600 5th Avenue South
Seattle, WA 98104
(206) 624-6248

Whole Foods Market
www.wholefoodsmarket.com
1026 NE 64th Street
Seattle, WA 98115
(206) 985-1500

University Seafood and Poultry
1317 Northeast 47th Street
Seattle, WA 98105
(206) 632-3900

Pike Place Fish in the Pike Place Market
www.pikeplacefish.com
86 Pike Street
Seattle, WA 98101
(206) 682-7181
You can request that they skip tossing your fish in the air; it is their specialty.

ONLINE SOURCES

Mundial, Inc.
www.MundialUSA.com
(800) 487-2224
Quality cutlery.

Browne Trading
Company
www.browne-trading.com
(800) 944-7848
*Select seafood, in addition to
smoked fish and caviar.*

Seafoods.com
www.seafoods.com
(877) 710-FINS
*Network of operations along
the eastern seaboard and Gulf
of Mexico.*

Please be aware that changes
to the above information
may have occurred since
publication.

GLOSSARY

Aji amarillo: Spicy Peruvian yellow pepper. Most commonly found as a jarred paste in South American markets.

Alfonso olive: Large blackish purple Spanish olive, often stuffed.

Basil oil: Oil infused with basil. It can be found in supermarkets.

Black truffle oil: Oil, often sunflower oil, infused with black truffles.

Bonito flakes: Dried fish shavings; found in Asian markets.

Causa: Peruvian potato terrine with layers of filling, usually served cold. Some versions are similar to shepherd's pie.

Chipotle pepper: Smoked jalapeño chile. Available canned in adobo sauce and dried. Fairly readily available in the ethnic sections of most groceries.

Coconut milk: Liquid prepared from the meat of fresh coconuts blended with water and strained (or heated and strained). It is most readily available canned.

Coconut water: Not coconut milk, but the thin juice found inside a fresh coconut. It can be found in the freezer section in Asian markets.

Coriander seeds: Actually the dried fruit of the cilantro plant, but with quite a different flavor than fresh cilantro leaves. The small, tan-colored seeds hold hints of caraway, sage, and citrus.

Corn nuts: Fried whole corn kernels with a crispy exterior and an almost powdery interior. Often used as a garnish in ceviches.

Culantro: Type of cilantro with a long, flat leaf. Also known in Spanish as *recao*.

Daikon radish: Oversized Asian radish with crisp, white flesh and a white or black exterior. It has an elongated root-like shape that can vary in size, and should be firm to the touch when purchased.

Dried porcini mushrooms: (pronounced pohr-CHEE-nee) Sometimes called cèpes. Prized wild mushrooms with a meaty texture and strong, earthy flavor. Most readily available in the United States

in dried form. Look for whole, not crushed, dried mushrooms with a light brown color.

Dried scallops: Called *kan pooi* or *koong yi chi* in Chinese. Hard, air-dried scallops from China or Japan with a salty, chewy bite. Prices vary depending on size. They are most easily available in Asian markets, typically sold out of glass jars.

Dried shrimp: Tiny dehydrated shrimp with intense flavor. Available whole or in powdered form at Asian markets.

Fish sauce: An intensely salty, brownish liquid made from fermented fish that is used in a variety of Southeast Asian cuisines. Called *nam pla* in Thai markets.

Galanga: Used as a seasoning, the creamy white flesh of this rhizome tastes like ginger and is available either fresh or dried (although this form is stronger in flavor) in Asian markets.

Huacatay: Black mint from Peru. Substitute fresh mint mixed with a leaf or two of cilantro. Look for this in

South American markets, but be prepared for a search as its fresh form is rare in the United States.

Huancaina: Peruvian spicy sauce made with cheese and eggs, traditionally served with potatoes.

Kaffir lime leaves: Shiny, dark green leaves from the kaffir lime tree of Southeast Asia and Hawaii. The fresh leaves have an intense floral, citrus aroma and can be found in Asian markets. More readily available dried.

Kecap manis: Also called "sweet soy," this is an Indonesian thick syrupy soy sauce sweetened with palm sugar and has spices such as star anise added. It is used in marinades and sauces and found in Asian markets.

Mandoline: Hand-held slicing machine with adjustable blades. Strongly recommended for thinly slicing ceviche ingredients. Available in specialty kitchenware stores.

Mustard oil: Pungent oil, with a horseradish-like heat, made from mustard seed. Found bottled in East Indian markets.

Nori furikake: Japanese condiment usually sprinkled over cooked rice consisting of a blend of sesame seeds, seaweed, dried ground fish, sugar, salt, and other flavorings. There are myriad flavor variations of this dried mixture ranging from spicy to salmon or wasabi flavored. It is found in Asian markets.

Opal basil: A variety of basil with a deep purple leaf. Look for it at specialty produce stores and farmers' markets.

Panca pepper: Sweet and spicy red chile pepper from Peru. It is most easily available canned in paste form in South American markets.

Papa: Spanish word for "potato."

Pequillo pepper: Small, red Spanish pepper. Available jarred in brine in Latin markets.

Plantain: *Plántano* in Spanish. A member of the banana family that is always used cooked. Sweet banana-like flavor with a brownish black skin when ripe; starchy in flavor with yellow skin that's freckled or spotted when semi-ripe; green skin in unripe state.

Ponzu: Japanese sauce typically a mix of rice vinegar, sake, soy sauce, seaweed, and bonito flakes and often used as a dipping sauce. It is most readily available bottled in Asian markets.

Pummelo: The world's largest citrus and a relative of the grapefruit, although with a thicker pith and skin. Pulp is uniquely crisp (similar to the seeds of a pomegranate) and sweeter and less acidic than grapefruit.

Quinoa: (pronounced KEEN-wah) A tiny, ancient grain-like seed, first cultivated by the Incas and still grown extensively in the Andean region of South America. High in protein and nutrients. Used like rice or couscous.

Saffron: Extremely expensive spice usually in thread or powdered form, the former being the whole crocus stigma from which the ground spice is made. Imparts a beautiful, bright yellow color and distinctive flavor to anything it is cooked with. Be cautious of imitation powders.

Sambal oelek: Tart Indonesian ground chile paste usually consisting of ground dried red chiles, vinegar, and sometimes sugar; used to add heat to a dish without adding other extra flavors. It can be purchased in Asian markets.

Serrano chiles: Small, thin peppers that range, depending on ripeness, from bright green, to red, to yellow. They are most easily available in Mexican groceries and come in a wide variety of forms: fresh, canned (in oil or pickled), dried, or in powdered form.

Serrano ham: Spanish salt-cured ham that is air-dried, similar to Italy's Parma ham.

Sherry: A fortified Spanish wine that ranges from dry and light (finos and manzanillas), to sweeter and darker (amontillados and olorosos). Use a reasonably priced, dry variety for cooking.

Shiso: Called Japanese basil or perilla, the green leaves of this member of the mint family have a fresh, herbal aroma and a distinctively Japanese flavor. Available fresh during summer and fall.

Thai basil: Lighter in color than regular basil and with a lemon-tinged aroma. Sometimes called hairy basil.

Thai chile: Tiny thin chile found in many Southeast Asian dishes; carries a lot of heat despite its size. Mostly found ripe and red, they can be green as well (similar to unripe jalapeños). Available in Asian markets and the produce section of some supermarkets.

Togarashi: Japanese dried spice blend used as a garnish for soups, noodles, or grilled meats; usually consists of ground dried red chile pepper, ground dried citrus peel, seaweed, ginger, and sometimes sesame seeds. It is readily available in Asian markets.

Turmeric: Spice of Asian origin with a slightly bitter, pungent flavor and a bright yellow-orange color similar to saffron. It is made from the root of a ginger-related plant and is a key ingredient in mustards and curries.

Valencia orange: A sweet orange that originated in Spain and Portugal, typically harvested from March through June.

Wasabi: Japanese horseradish with a bright green color. It is most easily found in Asian markets in powdered or paste form, rarely fresh.

Watercress: Small, peppery green from the mustard family.

Yuca: Root vegetable native to Africa, also known as cassava or manioc. Yuca (pronounced YOO-ka) is not to be confused with yucca (pronounced YUCK-a), a genus of plants in the agave family with sword-shaped leaves and white blooms. Yuca is a tuber and grows underground, like a potato. Commonly used for cooking throughout Latin America and the Caribbean. Elongated shape with a brown skin, a starchy white flesh, and a bland, slightly sweet potato–like flavor. To peel the long, tubular roots, hold in one hand and make broad slashing motions down the tuber with a large, heavy-duty knife. (A regular vegetable peeler will not work.)

Yuzu: Japanese citrus fruit with a flavor somewhere between lemon and lime. Its rind and juice are used to flavor soups, dressings, and marinades. Although not commonly found fresh in the United States, the frozen or bottled juice is available in Asian markets.

INDEX

CONVERSIONS

VOLUME

Formulas:

1 teaspoon = 4.93 milliliters

1 tablespoon = 14.79 milliliters / 3 teaspoons

1 cup = 236.59 milliliters / 16 tablespoons

1 liter = 202.88 teaspoons / 67.63 tablespoons / 4.23 cups

U.S.	Imperial	Metric
1 tablespoon	$^1/_2$ fl oz	15 ml
2 tablespoons	1 fl oz	30 ml
$^1/_4$ cup	2 fl oz	60 ml
$^1/_3$ cup	3 fl oz	90 ml
$^2/_3$ cup	5 fl oz ($^1/_4$ pint)	150 ml
$^3/_4$ cup	6 fl oz	180 ml
1 cup	8 fl oz ($^1/_3$ pint)	240 ml
$1^1/_4$ cups	10 fl oz ($^1/_2$ pint)	300 ml
2 cups (1 pint)	16 fl oz ($^2/_3$ pint)	480 ml
$2^1/_2$ cups	20 fl oz (1 pint)	600 ml
1 quart	32 fl oz ($1^2/_3$ pint)	1 l

LENGTH

Formulas:

1 inch = 2.54 cm   1 foot = .3 m / 12 inches

1 cm = .39 inch   1 m = 3.28 feet / 39.37 inches

Inch	Metric
$^1/_4$ inch	6 mm
$^1/_2$ inch	1.25 cm
$^3/_4$ inch	2 cm
1 inch	2.5 cm
6 inches ($^1/_2$ foot)	15 cm
12 inches (1 foot)	30 cm

TEMPERATURE

Formulas:

$^9/_5$ C + 32 = F   (F − 32) x $^5/_9$ = C

Fahrenheit	Celsius/Gas Mark
250°F	120°C / gas mark 1/2
275°F	135°C / gas mark 1
300°F	150°C / gas mark 2
325°F	160°C / gas mark 3
350°F	180 or 175°C / gas mark 4
375°F	190°C / gas mark 5
400°F	200°C / gas mark 6
425°F	220°C / gas mark 7
450°F	230°C / gas mark 8
475°F	245°C / gas mark 9
500°F	260°C

WEIGHT

Formulas:

1 ounce = 28.35 grams

1 pound = 453.59 grams /16 ounces

1 kilogram = 2.2 pounds

U.S./Imperial	Metric
$^1/_2$ oz	15 g
1 oz	30 g
2 oz	60 g
$^1/_4$ lb	115 g
$^1/_3$ lb	150 g
$^1/_2$ lb	225 g
$^3/_4$ lb	350 g
1 lb	450 g